In an age of great confusion about ( God's great love for His children. [ own experience as a parent, Greg A analogies that will lead readers to n. tionship with His children.

—Dr. David S. Dockery, President
Union University, Jackson, TN

Little Camden Ammons' dad has done a masterful job in opening the layers of his heart to help us begin to touch the hem of the garment of our Heavenly Father's love for us. I can enthusiastically endorse this volume to all people anywhere who long to know they are loved.

—Dr. O.S. Hawkins, President and CEO
Guidestone Financial Resources, Dallas, TX

In this insightful, autobiographical narrative Greg Ammons lays bare his soul as he speaks of his own love as a father against the greater backdrop of God's love for all humanity. You will be moved—sometimes to tears, sometimes to hilarious laughter—as he chronicles the journey he and Lisa are making now with Camden in discovering the depths of that love which will not let us go and which expresses itself anew every morning.

—Dr. Gary L. Hearon, Emeritus Executive Director
Dallas Baptist Association, Dallas, TX

Endearing reflections of how the birth of Greg Ammons' son changed his life lead to captivating truths of God as our Heavenly Father. What a compelling book for any parent and for everyone who desires to experience a deeper walk with the Lord.

—Ellen Dean, M.S., LPC, LMFT
Biblical Counseling and Ministries, Garland, TX

This book will encourage and give hope to those couples who want children but who have not been able to conceive a child. The concept of relating God's love to us and a father's love to his son brings a new and refreshing revelation of how God loves us unconditionally.

—Linda Dean, MEd. Premarital Specialist
Fielder Road Baptist Church Counseling Center, Arlington, TX

Published by
Hannibal Books
PO Box 461592
Garland, Texas 75046-1592
Copyright Greg Ammons 2007
All Rights Reserved
Printed in the United States of America
by Lightning Source, LaVergne, TN
Cover design by Greg Crull
Except where otherwise indicated, all Scripture taken from the Holy Bible,
*New International Version*, copyright 1973, 1978, 1984
by International Bible Society
ISBN 0-929292-46-4
Library of Congress Control Number: 2001012345

TO ORDER ADDITIONAL COPIES, SEE PAGE 237

# NOW MY E Y E SEES YOU

### WHAT A DOCTORATE DID NOT TEACH ME ABOUT GOD . . . MY SON DID

## GREG AMMONS

HANNIBAL BOOKS
www.hannibalbooks.com

# Acknowledgements

Special thanks to . . .

• My wife and best friend, Lisa, who takes such wonderful care of our son. My schedule is often very busy; she faithfully cares for Boomer. What a wonderful mother!

• My son, Camden, for giving up precious time with Daddy so I could write the manuscript for this book.

• My parents, the late Lee Roy and Joanne Ammons, for their love, care, provision, and devotion to me throughout their entire lives.

• My sister, Diana Clark, and her family. Boomer loves his Aunt Nanna and Uncle Bub. We love them, too.

• My brother, Steve Ammons, and his family. Boomer also loves his "Uncle Steve and Aunt Sheila Pickles." We love them, too.

• Special friends Larry and Carol Thompson of Iowa Park, TX. The Thompsons, along with their family, have been dear friends and have loved Camden as their own. We will always be indebted to you.

• Louis and Kay Moore of Hannibal Books for treating me as a friend as well as an author. You have taught me much about publishing with integrity.

• Barbara Smith, Heather Sanderson, and Shannon Fears, ministry assistants at the First Baptist Church of Garland, TX, who helped with the final stages of this project, on their own, in the midst of their busy schedules.

- Dr. Gary Cook, president of Dallas Baptist University, for his friendship and willingness to write the foreword to this book.
- Dr. Gary Hearon, Dr. David Dockery, Dr. O.S. Hawkins, Gov. Mike Huckabee, Ellen Dean, and Linda Dean for their support of this project.
- Friends who were willing to complete a survey concerning their children and their perception of the fatherhood of God: These were Dr. Tim Russell, Dr. Bruce Dane, Dr. John Duncan, Dr. Robert Prothro, Dr. Derrell Monday, Dr. Bob Sexton, Dr. Bobby Holt, Dr. Gary Hearon, Dr. Jerry Faught, Dr. Bill Buchanan, Dr. Gary Singleton, Dr. Jim Gatliff, Dr. Scott Willingham, Dr. Wayne Shuffield, Dr. Bailey Stone, Dr. Jerry Christopher, Dr. Michael Dean, Dr. Bobby Renfro, Dr. Chris Leibrum, and Dr. Ron Gunter.
- Clif, Lady B, and Jeff at The Texas Star Retreat Center for providing wonderful accommodations for me when I would retreat to write.
- Meagan Franks and Four Seasons Photography for some of the great photographs.
- The tremendous membership of the First Baptist Church of Garland. Serving God with such wonderful people is a pleasure.
- The remarkable membership of Faith Baptist Church of Iowa Park. You loved us dearly, prayed with us, rejoiced with us, and helped us prepare for the arrival of our son.
- Jesus Christ for changing my life, calling me into His vocational service, and blessing me with a wonderful wife and awesome little boy.

# Dedicated
## to

my wife, Lisa—God's wonderful helpmate
and one terrific mother

and

my son, Camden—who has brought
an unbelievable amount of joy to my life.

# Contents

# Foreword

Fifteen years ago, if you saw an older man and woman with children on the playground in the park, you would assume they were grandparents. Today this is not the case. Just as likely, many older men and women on playgrounds are called "Daddy" or "Mommy." Many more midlife parents are in our contemporary society than were in years past. In fact the number of first-time parents between the ages of 40 and 44 is the highest it has been since 1960 and has doubled since 1982.

First-time parents in their 40s have a unique vantage point on childrearing. For example, they are much more aware of their mortality. These parents are well aware of the fact they will not live forever. They possess a great desire to spend time with their children as well as to leave a legacy for them. Also bringing closure to the barren years is often difficult, as a new chapter of life opens for them. According to research, later-in-life, first-time fathers are more likely to play major roles in their children's upbringing.

Many of these first-time parents lived through years of childlessness, built a network of friends, and reached vocational milestones and even financial security but lacked the fulfillment of a child. They were well-aware of their fading youth and often wondered if the dream of rearing a child ever would be realized. Being more than 40 years old and having a child for the first time has its own unique challenges but also has its wonderful, unexpected pleasures.

Dr. Greg and Lisa Ammons are two of these midlife, first-time parents. After 18 years of marriage God answered their prayers and allowed them to bear a son, whom they named *Camden Isaac*. This book chronicles their journey of barrenness and the subsequent birth of their child. You will share in their experience of what having a child later in life is like. At 43-years old not many "firsts" are left. However Dr. Ammons shares in this book his poignant and inspiring viewpoint of being a first-time father at 43. He recounts the special and important bond formed between that of an older father and a son.

Dr. Ammons writes from the unique perspective of both a vocational minister and a first-time father later in life. The author serves as the senior pastor of the First Baptist Church in Garland, TX, and has been in vocational ministry for 27 years. He has earned theological degrees from two different institutions and holds a doctorate degree from Southwestern Baptist Theological Seminary. Having never been a father for 24 years of his ministry and then having a son impacted greatly his view of God. Ammons says, "I had known love only as a son for 43 years of my life. But, after Camden was born, I now know love from the perspective of a father. This experience has greatly enhanced my view of God."

The title of the book is taken from a powerful passage of Scripture (Job 42:5), in which Job declares that his experiences have changed his view of God. In *Now My Eye Sees You* you will read how being a first-time father later in life changed Dr. Ammons' concept of the fatherhood of God. You will read how, for this minister, basic doctrines of the Christian faith move into sharper focus. Dr. Ammons draws comparisons between his relationship with his son and that of his God in areas such as obedience and disobedience, spending time together, parental pain, teaching a child to walk, the sinful nature, and the powerful love of a father. Camden Isaac teaches his father what a doctorate degree in theology did not teach him. Dr. Ammons also writes of his relationship with his own father, now in heaven, and how it has impacted his role as a father as well.

To enhance the book Dr. Ammons conducted surveys of other vocational ministers who are parents and hold doctorate degrees in theology. The rich insight gained from his colleagues on how fatherhood changed their perspective of God is interspersed throughout the book.

Wherever you are in life's journey, you will find areas of this book which relate to you. As you read through the pages, you also will realize how much the Father loves you and desires intimate fellowship with you. *Now My Eye Sees You* will deepen your own view of the fatherhood of God as well as will introduce you to "Boomer", one special little boy God placed in the Ammons home.

Dr. Gary Cook, President
Dallas Baptist University

# Chapter 1

# We Are What?

At a popular Italian restaurant in Wichita Falls, TX, my wife, Lisa, and I sat across the table from each other. Our faces bore looks of disbelief. Our eyes met each others' as if to ask, "Is it really true?" As we awaited our food to be served, we experienced many different emotions—shock, disbelief, excitement, fright, to name a few. And we had many, many questions.

Some friends dropped by our restaurant table to say hello. They were members of nearby Faith Baptist Church in Iowa Park, TX, where I served as pastor. Before they left, we visited briefly and made small talk. We were not very talkative and were well aware that we looked somewhat shell-shocked. Later the friends told us that they noticed we were rather reserved and didn't seem to be ourselves. As they left, they commented, "Something really seemed wrong with Greg and Lisa today."

What our friends did not know and we had just discovered was that we were pregnant. The time was joyous but was also filled with disbelief and shock. After 18 years of marriage we had never been expecting. I was 43 years old and my wife was 39 years old. Now God appeared to have answered our prayer of many years and was giving us a child. *Is this news too good to be true?* Other questions surfaced. *Will Lisa be able to carry the child to full term? Are we too old to be first-time parents?*

# COULD IT BE TRUE?

A couple of weeks before our Italian-restaurant lunch, Lisa told me that she quite possibly was pregnant. We were cautiously optimistic and did not want to get our hopes up, just to have them dashed again. Lisa purchased a home-pregnancy test to find out whether her suspicion was correct. She tested, waited, and approached me with the news. "It was positive," she said. I questioned, "Are you sure? Why don't you try it again tomorrow? Perhaps a positive test could result for some other reason."

The next day Lisa took another home-pregnancy test. She walked into the living room and announced, "This one was positive, also. I think we are pregnant." Much like doubting Thomas, I said, "Let me see for myself." So I went to the bathroom, read the instructions carefully, checked the monitor stick, and said, "Well, according to this monitor, you are pregnant. Let me re-read the instructions." Nothing changed. Our home test showed a positive pregnancy.

Still skeptical and not wanting to get too excited too soon, I advised, "Why don't we schedule an appointment with the doctor and see what he says? Don't tell anyone about this until we find out for sure from the doctor." Lisa agreed; we kept the secret.

A few days later as we entered the examination room in the doctor's office, we were excited but skeptical. The nurse performed a pregnancy test and, in a wonderful Texas drawl, declared, "Yep, sure looks like you are pregnant." Lisa was thrilled, but I still was in the role of doubting Thomas. "How certain are you?" I asked. The nurse replied, "Fairly certain. More than 95 percent of the time this test is accurate. Occasionally we'll see an extenuating circumstance that results in a false positive, but I am fairly certain that you are going to have a baby." I quizzed further, "Could we have full certainty any other way?" The nurse hesitated, "If you'd like, we can perform a blood test which will allow us to know for sure." I agreed to the extra trouble and expense of performing a blood test. If we indeed were pregnant, I wanted to know absolutely and not be devastated, only to get my hopes up and then have them crushed.

My wife and I went across the street from the doctor's office to the laboratory, where technicians drew vials of Lisa's blood. They told us that we would not know the results of the blood work for a few days. They suggested we schedule another appointment with the doctor to get the results of the blood work. During the few days of waiting for the results, we were eager but said nothing to anyone—not even to our closest friends. Before we announced a pregnancy to anyone, we wanted to make absolutely certain.

Before the fateful doctor's visit at which we would find out with certainty of our pregnancy, the days seemed to crawl by. Apprehensively, when our names were called, Lisa and I entered the doctor's office. There the nurse informed us that the blood work had returned with 100-percent accuracy. We were pregnant. "We are what?" we asked. "Congratulations; you are pregnant." We were excited, thankful, fearful, and somewhat in shock. The journey had been a long one, but God had granted us the desire of our hearts. In shock we headed off to our favorite Italian restaurant to celebrate.


### OUR JOURNEY OF BARRENNESS

Our journey went back several years. On February 1, 1985, Lisa and I were married. As most young couples do, we discussed many aspects of our new life together. Of course one topic of much interest and debate was how many children we would like to have and, ideally, how long into the marriage we would wait before having children.

Many couples discuss these issues together, but rarely do they talk about their possible inability to conceive. Infertility affects six million couples in the United States each year—about 10 percent of all marriages.[1] Yet most couples believe it will never happen to them. *Of course, we will have children* usually is the thought of most couples. They usually do not even consider the possibility that infertility may affect them. We were just like other couples in thinking little of that likelihood.

Ideally we had wanted to wait about five years into our marriage to become parents. We believed that would be an adequate amount of time for us to develop a close bond between us before a child arrived. I would also have time to complete my theological studies, time for Lisa to complete her college degree, and time for us both to adjust to married life while I served as the pastor of Floyd Baptist Church near Greenville, TX. However we had no idea that our journey of childlessness would extend into 18 years of marriage.

After some time we decided that we would undergo testing to see if we could find a reason why we could not conceive. Our testing began with me. When I was only 18 years old, I had contracted Rocky Mountain Spotted Fever from a tick bite to the lower leg. This powerful disease overwhelmed my young body and almost took my life. It affected me in various ways; through the years we often wondered if perhaps this disease made fathering a child impossible for me. After extensive research a local urologist declared that I indeed was able to father a child.

Next Lisa and I decided to contact a reproductive specialist in the Dallas-Fort Worth area. We both underwent testing and had in-depth discussions with the specialist about the options available to us. First the doctor stated that she saw no apparent reason why we could not bear children. However she told us that almost 25 percent of all infertility in couples unable to conceive is unexplained from a medical perspective. "We may never know medically why you cannot conceive a child," the doctor told us. One option available to us was in-vitro fertilization. The process was explained to us; we received literature and were told to go home to discuss this possibility. We did just that and made the decision a matter of prayer between us.

In-vitro fertilization is a process in which the sperm and egg are mixed in a laboratory and then are implanted into the female for her to carry. This procedure is attempted 100,000 times per year in our country and is successful almost 50 percent of the time in women who are 35 years of age or younger. Since the inception of in-vitro fertilization almost three decades ago, three-million babies have been conceived in this manner.[2] For many couples it is a wonderful option.

However Lisa and I completely agreed about the approach we would take. Neither of us believed that in-vitro fertilization was a viable option for us. We believed that we would simply continue praying about being parents. Almost simultaneously we said: "If God wants us to have a child, then God is well able to give us one if it is His will." So our approach was to pray and not utilize any type of artificial reproduction means, including fertility pills. This decision made the pregnancy announcement even more of a cause for praise from our lips!

### WHAT'S IN A NAME?

The first few weeks of pregnancy were an interesting time for both Lisa and me. We saw no outward signs that new life was growing inside of my wife, so believing this development was still difficult for us. *Had we read the home pregnancy test correctly? Had the doctor read the results of the blood work correctly? Were we victims of some cruel mistake in which the doctor's office would call back and tell us that something had been read incorrectly and we were not pregnant? Was this a dream from which we would awaken and discover that we still were barren? Would Lisa be able to carry a baby to full term?* Because of her age, Lisa's was considered to be a "high-risk" pregnancy. *Surely God would not allow us to become pregnant after all of these years and then lose the baby, would He?* From time to time during the first few weeks of our pregnancy each of these questions would surface in my mind.

As the weeks progressed, outward signs of pregnancy began to show. When Lisa first began to "pooch" to some degree, we would examine her stomach and ask, "Do you think it's getting any larger?" As crazy as this may sound, we would simply sit and rub her stomach. What a sight—two adults, one in his 40s and the other almost at that age, just sitting on the couch at night and rubbing a pregnant stomach! After 18 years of marriage we were still in disbelief that this wonderful dream was actually true. However, after a few months, we clearly saw that new life indeed was growing inside of Lisa.

Next we faced the task of naming our child. Because of a sonogram, which I will explain in more detail in the next chapter, we knew the gender of our child. Naming our son was a much more daunting task than we had envisioned. We bought two books which suggested names for a baby. Just the process of purchasing these books was exciting and seemed almost surreal to us. Each evening we would sit down and peruse the books, call out names, and then watch the other's reaction. The time was fun for both of us. We couldn't believe that God actually was allowing us to experience this moment It was exciting, but we also felt the weight of our decision.

We wanted to give our son a name of deep significance. Ours was a journey of faith; we wanted his name to reflect our experience. We also wanted his name to reflect the deep faith we possessed in Christ. We thought of possibly naming him after one of our fathers. Lisa's father, James, had died years earlier at a young age. My father, Lee Roy, was ill with cancer and would not live to see our son reared. However we could not agree on a name we liked which would honor one of these relatives.

We settled on the name *Camden* as a first name. It was unique, yet we both liked the sound of it. When he was born on July 4, we knew for certain this would be our son's name. In Old English the name *Camden* means "freedom." It was a perfect name for our son born on Independence Day, but it also represented the freedom we both enjoy as believers in Jesus Christ.

Jesus said in John 8:32, "*If the son sets you free, then you are free indeed.*" Lisa and I enjoy the political freedom we have as Americans, yet our greatest freedom is spiritual and occurs through a relationship with Jesus Christ. We both knew that the double meaning of *freedom* which Camden represented was the perfect name for him.

The middle name was my idea; Lisa agreed. One of my favorite stories from Scripture is the Genesis account of the birth of Isaac. For many years Abraham and Sarah were childless. Abraham received God's promise (Gen. 12:1-3) but had no male heir to carry out the promise. In Genesis 18 God sent men to the home of Abraham and Sarah to inform them that they would have a child. When she heard the men's announcement, Sarah was in the back of the home and laughed at the thought that she would, in her old age, bear a child.

When God's promise was fulfilled in Genesis 21 and Sarah gave birth to a son, they named him *Isaac*, which meant "laughter." A variation of meaning for *Isaac* was "joy." I thought *Isaac* was the perfect middle name for our son since God blessed us in our "old age" with a little boy. We prayed that he would bring us many days of laughter and joy. God answered that prayer as well. Our son certainly has done that! His name would be *Camden Isaac Ammons*.

Months before he was born a nickname for our son developed quickly. His nickname is *Boomer*. To this day many close friends and family members still call our son *Boomer*. It all began with some good-natured teasing I received from our University of Texas friends. My wife and I have always been staunch fans of the University of Oklahoma; its fight song is entitled, "Boomer Sooner." My UT friends jokingly wanted me to name my son after the capital of Texas, where the university is situated. They joked, "Name your son *Austin*. It would be a beautiful name. *Austin Ammons*. Perfect!" I jokingly responded, "No, I think we'll call him Boomer." Well, the nickname stuck! Six months before he was born, family and friends began calling him *Little Boomer*. *Camden "Boomer" Ammons* was now well on his way.


**THE BIRTH**

Our due date was June 27, 2003. As this due date approached, Lisa's weekly doctor's exams grew more frustrating. "You are not any closer than you were last week. You may go past your due date," the physician advised us. I was apprehensive about the birth; the delay added to my apprehension. *Would I be a good father?* I was the youngest of three children and hadn't really been around babies before. *How would I deal with things?* As the due date approached, I had many questions. Lisa was weary physically and eager to deliver the child. At our home, as the birth grew near, we had many late nights in which we would lie awake and talk about our feelings.

During Lisa's physical examination on July 2, the doctor told us that he believed he must induce labor since she had gone a few days past her due date and because of her age. That afternoon we were to check into the Wichita General Hospital in Wichita Falls; the induction would begin. As we packed our clothes and left for the hospital, the reality of the entire experience began to set in. After our 18 years of marriage, God had truly blessed us. Lisa was able to carry the baby to full term. As a couple we were leaving our home in the way we had done hundreds of times before during 18 years of marriage. But we knew that this time our return home would be different. We would return as a family of three rather than two. The emotion I felt was overwhelming.

We settled into our hospital room for the evening; the drugs were administered to induce labor. The next day seemed to be the day we were going to have a long-awaited baby. Neither of us slept much through the night. A sinus infection kept me from resting well. We both were excited and apprehensive.

Early the next morning, July 3, family and friends gathered in the delivery waiting area of Wichita General Hospital. I served as the senior pastor of Faith Baptist Church in nearby Iowa Park. Many members dropped by the hospital to visit or called on the telephone. We were most appreciative and felt much love and support. However, the delivery was slow in happening.The morning hours went by; Lisa still had dilated only to two centimeters. She was given an epidural; her pain was managed, but she was slow to deliver.

By mid-afternoon, she was still only at a stage two of dilation; the doctor became somewhat concerned. Again, because of Lisa's age, the concern was more acute. Discussion began about taking our son by cesarean section. By late afternoon, the doctor said if she did not make progress quickly, then she would go into surgery that evening.

Around 5 p.m., a nurse checked Lisa and notified me in the waiting room that Lisa now had progressed to a stage five of dilation. The birthing process should be moving along soon. Now I became really nervous! I went to Lisa's bedside to hold her hand and do my part, which I had practiced in the childbirthing classes. The time had arrived to put my training into practice.

At 12 minutes past midnight on July 4, 2003, Camden Isaac Ammons made his entrance into the world. I hoped Camden was physically well and totally healthy, but at that moment, that wasn't my greatest thought. No matter his condition, I loved him instantly. He was here. I had a son! Three years later as I write about this wonderful experience, my eyes are filled with tears. This moment was a culmination of years of frustration and questions yet faithfulness to God. Our Heavenly Father indeed had blessed us and given us a son. At the age of 43 and after 18 years of marriage, God answered my prayers and allowed me to be a father. The moment was overwhelming.

## THE ADVENTURE BEGINS

Two days later we brought our son home from the hospital. I'll never forget the day. We went home in late afternoon; our Pontiac Grand Prix was literally packed with flowers, gifts, supplies, two "green" parents, one beautiful boy, and a lot of love. We made the short drive of 10 miles from the hospital to our home. As I drove with our son in the vehicle, I was extremely cautious. As I crept along, one vehicle zipped by me on the freeway; I thought, "Why are you driving so fast? Don't you know I have a baby in here?" Being a protective parent already had begun!

When we arrived at home, what occurred is one of those moments in life that freeze in time in your mind. I still can recall every detail as if things were happening yesterday. I drove into the drive knowing that the neighbors would be watching. As Lisa carefully took Camden inside, I unloaded everything out of the car. On the front lawn I proudly displayed a yard sign the hospital personnel gave us. The sign read, "It's a Boy!" As I placed the sign on the lawn, my mind raced to Genesis 21. I thought of Abraham. What a moment!

I went inside the house where Lisa was simply walking from room to room and holding our new bundle of joy. We introduced him to each room before the three of us bowed and prayed together. After about 20 minutes, Lisa and I looked at each other quizzically and both asked simultaneously, "What do we do now?" We felt totally inadequate. We both wished the hospital nurses could have gone home with us to give us some instruction. We both asked where the owner's manual was for our new addition. We both wondered whether we were up to the task.

Little did we realize that this would be the first of many such moments in which we would ask, "Now what?" It would be the first of many times in which we would feel inadequate for the task and would pray for wisdom. After 18 years of marriage we stood there looking at each other and then looking down at our son. Everything seemed surreal. The lessons I would learn about my Heavenly Father over the next three years would be life-changing. The adventure had only begun.

## "NOW MY EYE SEES YOU"

The title of the book is derived from one of my favorite passages of Scripture. It also applies to my experiences with Camden. As I began the process of writing this work, *Now My Eye Sees You* seemed to be the perfect title.

I'm sure you have heard the story. Job was a man who was blameless and upright, feared God, and shunned evil (Job 1:1). Job was blessed with seven sons and three daughters. He was also blessed with great possessions. Scripture tells us that Job possessed many camels, sheep, oxen, and donkeys. He was one of the greatest men in the East.

One day Satan appeared before the Lord as a heavenly council convened and a conversation ensued. (Job 1:6). *"Have you considered my servant Job?"* God asked. *"There is none like him on the earth, a blameless and upright man who shuns evil,"* the Lord commented. I'm interested in the fact that God almost was bragging on his son as a proud father would!

Satan answered and inquired, *"Does Job fear God for nothing? You have blessed the work of his hands and his possessions have increased . . . .. But, now, stretch out your hand against all that he has and he will surely curse you to your face."* God allowed the devil to attack Job, but he could not touch his person (Job 1:12).

Through a series of catastrophes under Satan's onslaught Job lost his 10 children, all of his possessions, and his health. Yet in all of it Job did not accuse God of treating him badly (Job 1:22).

Job's three friends approached him and began to philosophize about the matters in an effort to understand why these negative events occurred. Eliphaz, Bildad, and Zophar told Job that in his life he surely had unconfessed sin and that God was punishing him. Job insisted that he knew of none. He was perplexed as to why such calamity had befallen him. From Chapter 2 through Chapter 31 the conversation between Job and his three friends raged back and forth.

In Chapter 32 Job's young friend named Elihu joined the conversation. He observed that wisdom is a gift from God that doesn't necessarily happen with age, so he offered his insight. "Perhaps," Elihu opined, "that it was not Job's sin which brought this adversity. Maybe a dynamic is at work here that is unseen to the human eye. Perhaps God is using this event to do a greater work of which we are all unaware. And, when Job emerges through the adversity, he will see God in a different light."

I find interesting the fact that during the entire conversation between Job and his four friends the book of Job does not record one comment from God. The Lord said nothing until Chapter 38! When the Lord finally spoke, he offered no explanation—only a challenge to trust and believe. Wouldn't simply explaining to Job about the conversation earlier with Satan have been much easier? At times explanations are not needed. At such times simply trust God. In that we find our strength.

For four chapters the Lord asked Job a series of questions (Job 38-41). Through God's questioning Job was humbled. Finally in Chapter 42 Job responded to God and confessed his lack of understanding. Yet these incidents had given Job a different insight into his God.

In a beautiful statement in Chapter 42:5, Job said, "*I have heard of you by the hearing of the ear, but now my eye sees you.*" Job was confessing that before his experiences, he knew God partially. However, after his experiences, Job realized that he knew God in a completely different way. He almost seems to have heard of God before the experiences but actually had seen God after them. Now his eye saw Him.

# NOW MY EYE SEES HIM

Just before his third birthday Camden was scheduled for a visit to the doctor's office. Lisa and I were explaining to our son that we were taking him to the physician for a routine examination. We assured him that he would not be harmed and that the doctor simply wanted to look at him. "In fact," we surmised, "he may even give you a sucker or a sticker for your visit today." During the course of the conversation Lisa mentioned to Camden, "Did you know that Daddy is a doctor?" She knew he was incapable of understanding the difference between a physician and a theological doctorate but simply thought she would have some fun with him. After Lisa asked her introspective question, our son laughed until he hardly could catch his breath, glanced over at me, and then exclaimed, "You're not a doctor! You're a daddy!"

Little did Camden realize that he had stated exactly how I intend to relate to my son throughout the course of his life. My great desire is to be a role model, mentor, and friend to my son while, of course, being a parent. I want to be a father-figure to him just as my father was to me. And I want to be the ultimate example of unconditional love, just as my Heavenly Father continues to be to me. Camden indeed had stated it correctly. To him I am not a doctor; I am a daddy!

I am in the process of preparing a unique picture sequence to decorate my office at the church. I am getting a set of three pictures to be placed in one long, continuous frame to sit on my shelf. This idea occurred to me through reading the well-known Christian author, Tim Kimmel.[3] The first photograph in the sequence will be of the home of my birth in Durant, OK. The final photograph in the sequence will be of Highland Cemetery in Boswell, OK—the location of my burial when I die. The middle picture in the sequence will be of my wife and little boy. The picture frame will be a daily reminder of the place my physical life began, where it will end, and what is important between these two monumental events in my life.

God is the most important part of my life. My relationship with my Heavenly Father through Jesus Christ is what truly motivates me each day. He has given me two beautiful people with whom to share life; this picture frame depicts His wonderful blessings to me. Through these two special people—my wife and son—I view a microcosm of my relationship with God.

Years before Camden entered my life, I knew God personally. At age 9 I accepted Jesus Christ as my personal Savior and Lord. At age 19 I surrendered to God's call on my life to vocational ministry.

Every degree I earned in higher education was in the field of theology. In 1982 I received from Oklahoma Baptist University a bachelor of arts degree in religion. In 1986 I received from Southwestern Baptist Theological Seminary a master of divinity degree with emphases in missions and evangelism. In 1988 from the same seminary I received a doctor of ministry degree with emphases in pastoral ministry and theology. For many years I studied about God in the classroom.

My ears heard of Him. Yet my entire theological education was received while I was not in the role of a father personally. However, after I had a son of my own, my perception of the fatherhood of God changed. I felt as though now my eyes had seen Him. Not only was I learning about God through my little boy, but I was learning more about myself as well.

In no way am I comparing what Job endured to what I experienced through 18 years of childlessness. Job suffered calamity I have never known. However his experiences changed his perception of His Father. And so did mine. Once I became a father, my understanding of my Heavenly Father drastically changed and deepened.

From what I understand, I am not alone. As a part of the research for this book I interviewed 20 vocational ministers who have children. Each person I interviewed holds a doctorate degree in theology and serves in vocational ministry. Together this unique group combines 400 years of vocational ministry. The average length of each minister's ministry spans 36 years. The number of children these ministers enjoy ranges from two to five. The age of the children also varies greatly. The youngest minister's child is 6 years old, with the oldest child being 50 years of age. Most of these ministers (84 percent) bore their children either during or after their theological education. Their insights both as fathers and ministers are valuable to me.

I probed each of them to find out how their perception of the fatherhood of God changed once they bore children. I wanted to know what they perceived as the greatest challenges, as well as the most wonderful blessings, of being a father. Also I wanted to know how their perception of the attributes of God changed once they had children. Throughout the course of this book I will share these findings.

## THE ANALOGY OF A FATHER AND SON

A class of first-grade students in Sunday School was asked to draw a picture of how they thought God looked. Their drawings were quite revealing and sometimes amusing. One child depicted God in the form of a brightly-colored rainbow. Another child pictured Him as an old man descending from a cloud. Still another child drew God with a striking resemblance to Superman. The best snapshot of God was from another child who said, "I don't know what God looks like, so I just drew a picture of my daddy."[4]

As a father I feel a great responsibility to reflect God to my son. By peering at the same characteristics in his earthly father I want him to have a wonderful, loving, positive image of His Heavenly Father. The ministers interviewed for this book reflected a similar desire.

Several of the ministers mentioned the example they set before their children and how it affects them. They mentioned presenting an accurate picture of God to their children as one of their greatest parental challenges. One minister I respect greatly reflected, "My father, who is 82 years old now, is a wonderful picture to me of my Heavenly Father. He always has portrayed God accurately to me. I want to be that same picture of God to my children." Perhaps this is what our Heavenly Father had in mind when He used the analogy of a father and son to describe His relationship with His people.

Throughout Scripture God called Himself a *Father* and His people *sons*. The prophet Isaiah declared, *Doubtless you are our Father*, (Isa. 63:16) while the Apostle Paul quoted this same verse in Ephesians 4:6. As he foretold the Messiah's arrival (Isa. 9:6), Isaiah also used the term *Everlasting Father* to describe God's Son (Isa. 9:6). Through the Old Testament prophet Jeremiah, God said, *"For I am a Father to Israel and Ephraim is my firstborn"* (Jer. 31:9). On two different occasions New Testament writers quoted Old Testament passages in which God declared, *"I will be a Father to you and you shall be My sons . . ."* (2 Cor. 6:18; Heb. 1:5).

God also couched His relationship with His people in the context of that of a father and son. In Genesis 12 He called Abraham to be the *Father* of Israel. The Israelites were known as the *children of God*. Our Heavenly Father then established His people during a time and in a region in which the society

29

was patriarchal. Blessings were passed along through the lineage of the father.

Nearly 2,800 times in Scripture the words *father* and *son* are used. The Apostle Paul wrote of how intimate our relationship with God is when he stated, *For you are all sons of God through faith in Christ Jesus* (Gal. 3:26). Yet Paul went on to say that we not only are sons but heirs of all things (Gal. 4:7).

I'm interested that God used the analogy of a father and a son to describe His relationship with redeemed humanity. To capture the essence of our relationship with Him, God could have used one of several other analogies. He could have used the analogy of a master and slave. He could have used the analogy of an employer and an employee. He could have used the analogy of a sovereign (which He is) and a peasant. Yet when describing the most important relationship ever, God chose to use the analogy of a father and son. Why? Of all of the analogies God could have used, why did He choose this one?

I am uncertain as to all of the reasons why God used the father/son motif to describe His dealings with His people. In fact I am convinced that only when I get to heaven will I understand this powerful analogy in its fullness. However, on July 4, 2003, I began to understand the concept of father and son in a different way. Now that I was a father, I began to understand the Heavenly Father better. In the following pages I will share with you what I learned about God and how my perception of the fatherhood of God changed—not from a textbook but from a brown-haired, brown-eyed little boy.

# Chapter 2

# The Incredible Love of a Father

The aspect of fatherhood which surprised me the most was the depth of love I would have for my child. I knew I would love my child deeply. I knew this love would be different than the other kinds of love which I had experienced. Yet as a father the immense depth of this love surprised and overtook me!

My entire life I had heard that a parent's love for a child is incredible. When they were rearing me, my parents tried to tell me about parental love, but they couldn't put it into words. "Just wait until you have a child of your own. Then you will understand," they would say. Later, when I was still childless, I heard from other parents about unconditional love. They described to me the depth of love they felt for their children. Yet in all honesty, I didn't understand it. I preached on parenting and family roles, but I didn't really understand the depth of a parent's love for a child. I often wondered why parents did certain things for their children. I did not understand. When I was childless and serving as pastor of churches, members would describe to me the depth of love they felt for their children. "Pastor, you really don't know until you have a child of your own." They were correct. I really did not understand.

After Camden's birth, I understood better what others had been trying to tell me. Immediately I felt a depth of love which I had not experienced previously. I knew God loved me. I had experienced His love. But this love for my child was different. Previously all I had known was unconditional love from the viewpoint of a child. From a son's perspective I certainly had experienced a father's love. Yet now, for the first time, I experienced a father's love from the father's perspective. And it was different.

### HOW DO YOU DESCRIBE IT?

William Gladstone announced to the House of Commons the death of Princess Alice. As he did so Gladstone related the touching story of her death. The daughter of the princess was seriously ill with diphtheria. Doctors instructed the princess not to kiss her daughter, or else her own life would be endangered. On one occasion the daughter was struggling to breathe. The mother instinctively grabbed her daughter and cradled her in her arms. "Please kiss me, mother," the young girl pleaded. Without hesitation, the princess tenderly kissed her daughter. As a result of the loving action, the princess contracted diphtheria and died a few days later.[1]

As a father, I now understand why the princess would take such an action. Unconditional love is amazing to watch in action. Yet how do you describe, in words, the unconditional love a parent has for his or her child? It truly is indescribable. This was the task of the biblical writers as they attempted to pen words to describe God's love.

Scripture attempts to convey God's love in terms we can best understand. Throughout Scripture God speaks of His love for His children. The word *love* is used 323 times in Scripture. It is a major theme running throughout God's Word.

The words chosen by biblical writers to convey God's love for His people are rich in meaning. In the Old Testament the most common Hebrew word for *love* is *ahab*. It is the kind of love expressed toward human beings, as opposed to other objects. Love for a human was to be a higher kind of love. In the Old Testament *Ahab* is used 195 times. A lesser-used Old Testament word for *love* is powerful as well. In the Old Testament the word *chashaq* is used only 11 times. It is replete with richness, as it means to be attached deeply to an object or to long deeply for someone. God's wonderful love is described in the Old Testament as a deep attachment or an intense longing.

In the New Testament, Greek words are also deep in meaning in describing God's love for humanity. The most common word the Greek language uses to describe God's unconditional love is *agape*. It is used 109 times in the New Testament and means "to love deeply." *Agape* also carries the idea of being well-pleased or contented with someone.


## A HEAD-SCRATCHING STORY

One specific, biblical narrative took on a completely different significance to me once Camden was born. I had preached many messages from Genesis 22. For 24 years before my son's birth I proclaimed spiritual principles from this wonderful text. I loved the passage because I always thought it was a beautiful picture of Jesus and the wonderful love of a father. But again, my viewpoint was from the perspective of a son. Now, as a father, this passage was troublesome to me.

You may remember the story. In Genesis 12 God spoke to Abraham and commanded him to leave his country, people, and father's household to go to an unknown land. God promised him, "*I will make you into a great nation and will bless you. I will make your name great and you will be a blessing*"

(Gen. 12:2). The problem with this promise was that Abraham was 75 years old and had no male heir because Sarah, his wife, was barren. I am certain that Abraham wondered how God would keep this wonderful promise when he did not have a male offspring to carry his name. In obedience Abraham left Haran as God commanded and simply trusted Him.

In Genesis 18 God sent three visitors to Abraham and Sarah to encourage them and to announce to them that they would become pregnant and have a baby boy. From the back of the home Sarah heard the conversation and laughed at the prospect of having a child in their old age.

Yet in Genesis 21, the unthinkable happened. God was gracious to Sarah; she became pregnant and delivered a baby boy. They named him *Isaac*, which meant "laughter." Once again this was the reason that Lisa and I named our little boy *Camden Isaac*. We prayed that he would bring us the same joy and laughter in our "old age" as Abraham and Sarah's son had to them.

Then the crucible of Genesis 22 appeared. Wow, what an unbelievable challenge Abraham faced! God later spoke to Abraham and told him to take his son, Isaac, whom he loved, to the mountains. This was not to be a recreational trip. He was to take Isaac to Mount Moriah and to sacrifice him as a burnt offering to the Lord.

Abraham must have had many different emotions running through his body. I can hear his thoughts: "Lord, you called me out of Haran; I obeyed. Father, I was childless; you blessed me miraculously. And, now, Lord, you are asking me to sacrifice to you the only apparent way of fulfilling your promise to me."

Also Abraham surely felt the same love toward Isaac as I do toward my Isaac. When the Lord used the phrase "*whom thou lovest*" (Gen. 22:2 KJV), God reminded the patriarch of his deep love for Isaac. This must have been a difficult command to obey.

Yet to Abraham's credit Scriptures does not tell us about any doubt, hesitation, or disobedience on the part of this great patriarch. Early the next morning after God's command, Abraham rose early, saddled his donkey, and began making the long, painful journey toward Mount Moriah to sacrifice Isaac.

Along the way Isaac wondered aloud the purpose of the journey. We are not told Isaac's age, but he apparently was old enough to question the purpose of the trip. *"Father, we have the fire and wood, but where is the lamb for the burnt offering?"* Abraham replied, *"God will provide himself the lamb for the burnt offering"* (Gen. 22:7-8). So they continued the journey.

When they reached the location, Abraham told his servants to remain at the bottom of the mountain while the father and son went to the top and worshiped. When the father and son reached the summit, Abraham bound his son, Isaac, with a rope and placed him on top of the wood. He was prepared to sacrifice the love of his life to the Lord.

How could Abraham do this? How could Abraham sacrifice his Isaac?

Could I have done this? I love my Camden Isaac with a passion. I had always viewed this passage and preached it from the perspective of a son. But now, as a father, the sheer magnitude of what Abraham was asked to do overwhelms me.

We know how the story ends. The knife was raised skyward. Abraham's bundle of love was lying beneath. This man of God was ready to plunge the blade into his passion and promise. At just the point of Abraham's obedience, an angel appeared and declared, *"Abraham, Abraham, don't touch the young man! Don't lay a hand on him. Now, I know that you fear God, because you have not withheld your only son from me*" (Gen. 22:11-12). Just then, Abraham noticed behind him that a ram was caught in a thicket by its horns. Indeed, God had provided a burnt offering.

This is a moving passage as I contemplate what kind of love would actually have plunged the knife. God loves me infinitely more than I love Camden. You see, just like me, God also had only one Son. He was willing to lay him on the cross and sacrifice Him for me.

One of the most powerful songs I have heard since Camden's birth is entitled "Isaac." It was written by Bonnie Keen in 1998 after she had experienced some personal difficulties. The words are powerful as I contemplate this story:

> I have a prayer as pure as gold,
> That where you lead me, I will go.
> And I'll not miss the impassioned plea,
> When your sweet Spirit calls to me.
>
> And in that hour, and in that time,
> When I must lose my will in Thine.
> O my allegiance will be found,
> The day I lay my Isaac down.
>
> Grant me a faith beyond all doubt,
> Whose flames of hope cannot burn out.
> Let mercy flow and grace abound,
> The day I lay my Isaac down.
>
> Sweet lamb of love, most blessed friend,
> Nailed to the altar for my sin.
> Where in my place God's Son was bound,
> The day he laid His Jesus down.

Each idol vain is now laid bare,
His suffering cross my heart will share.
Earth kingdoms fall without a sound,
The day I lay my Isaac down.[2]

The story of Abraham and Isaac truly makes you scratch your head and ask, "Why?" The only answer I can find rests in the same indescribable feeling I had when I first picked up my son in the hospital nursery. *Love*. True, unconditional *love*.

## GOD'S LOVE IN THE OLD TESTAMENT

Many Christians think of the Old Testament as law rather than love. It is perceived as a harsh, condemning, and strict law. Many people believe that very little love, if any, is expressed in the Old Testament. Yet God's wonderful love for His people is a theme running throughout all of Scripture, including the Old Testament.

Surprisingly the word *love* appears almost as much in the Old Testament as it does the New Testament. This powerful word appears 124 times in the Old Testament, as opposed to 157 times in the New Testament. Repeatedly God assured His people of His unfailing love for them. In the Pentateuch the word *love* is mentioned 24 times. In Exodus 34 the Lord assured the Israelites that He was rich in unfailing love (verse 6) and that His love extended to thousands of generations (verse 7). In Deuteronomy God calmed the fears of the Israelites by reminding them of His love and asking for their love in return (Deut. 10:12; 11:1; 30:6). Yes, God's love is clearly visible in the midst of law.

Historical narratives in the Old Testament also record God's love for His people. God assured the Israelites that His

love for them was steadfast in spite of both positive and negative leadership from the kings. In 1 Kings 10:9 the narrative
speaks of God's eternal love for Israel. In 1 Chronicles the
Lord assured the Israelites, "*I will be a Father to you and you
will be a son to me*" (1 Chron. 16:41). An oft-repeated phrase
in the historical narratives of the Old Testament is *his faithful
love endures forever (*1 Chron. 17:13 is an example*).*

Wisdom literatures also records God's love for His people.
The word *love* appears 70 different times in this section of
Scripture. The wisdom books speak frequently of God's love.
They were written by children of God reflecting on the love of
their Father. Evidently the Old Testament saints were confi-
dent and assured of the fatherly love of their God.

As the Old Testament closes, judgment appears to be the
primary theme of the prophets. Yet 26 different times through
both major and minor prophets, God told His people of His
love for them. The Old Testament prophets were known primarily for messages of doom and impending judgment. But in
the midst of doom always was hope. Each Old Testament
prophet offered some measure of hope and love. God's love is
a thread that is clearly visible as it runs throughout the entire
Old Testament.


## GOD'S LOVE IN THE NEW TESTAMENT

You may expect to see God's love more in the New
Testament than you do in the Old Testament. The perception
of many people is that the Old Testament reflects law and
judgment, while the New Testament tempers it with love.
Already we have seen that God's love is expressed in the Old
Testament. Indeed that characteristic is evident in the New
Testament as well—some 157 times.

In the gospels Jesus often spoke of God's love. In the Sermon on the Mount He spoke of the need to love even our enemies (Mt. 5:44) Jesus quoted the Shema from Deuteronomy 6:5 when He was speaking with the Pharisees in Matthew 22. The Savior told the religious leaders, *"Thou shalt love the Lord with all your heart, and with all your soul and with all your mind"* (Mt. 22:37 KJV).

Perhaps our Lord's teaching on love reaches its zenith in the third chapter of John's gospel when Jesus said, *"For God so loved the world that he gave his only begotten son that whosoever believeth in him shall not perish but have everlasting life"* (verse 16). Jesus expressed God's love as a Father on other occasions as well. One such occasion was in Luke 15 in the parable of the prodigal son, in which the profound love of a father was expressed. As he welcomed the return of his son regardless of the circumstances, the father's love was unchanging.

Throughout his letters to various churches and individuals Paul continued the imagery of God as a loving father. In two outstanding chapters in Romans, Paul spoke of God's wonderful love for us. In chapter 5, verse 8, the great apostle declared that God "commended his love toward us in that while we were yet sinners Christ died for us." Also, in Romans 8:35-39, he spoke of how God's love was so strong for His children that absolutely nothing could separate us from it.

Other writings in the New Testament show the fatherly love of God. James spoke of love as the royal law (Jas. 2:8). Peter declared that Christians are to love the brotherhood (1 Pet. 2:17). Both apostles viewed our love as a reflection of the unconditional love God has for us. The most poignant picture of love in the General Epistles appeared in 1 John. The apostle told us that God loves us so deeply that He bestowed on us the designation of *sons*: *Behold, what manner of love the father has bestowed upon us, that we should be called the sons of God* (1 John 3:1). John also went so far as to define God as *love* (1 John. 4:8). The very definition of the love I feel for Camden is that of God Himself!

The ministers I interviewed for this book often spoke of the love of God. They mentioned how being a father deepened their view of God's love for them. I asked the group, "How did your perception of the Fatherhood of God change once you became a father?" An overwhelming number of ministers responded with references to the love of God. One minister opined, "Knowing how much I loved my child and then thinking about how much God must love me just floored me. It made me aware how difficult God's sending His Son to actually die for someone else must have been. I couldn't do that."

A certain medieval monk announced that he would preach the following Sunday evening on the topic of the love of God. The eager congregation gathered as the shadows fell and the light faded from the cathedral windows. In the darkness of the altar in the center of the platform, the monk lit a candle and carried it to the crucifix. First he illumined the crown of thorns. Next he carried the light to the two wounded hands and then to the marks of the spear wound in Jesus' side. In the silent hush the monk blew out the candle and left the chancel. It was a powerful message on the love of God, yet a word was never spoken. God's love is ultimately portrayed on the cross of Jesus. Love is an action word.[3]

## MY EARLY LOVE FOR CAMDEN

It began when I first knew for certain that we were pregnant. I found myself loving this unborn child immensely. Lisa was careful to watch her diet, get plenty of rest, and observe all of the other suggestions given to expectant mothers. Our love and care of Camden began very early. As I thought about him, I had overwhelming thoughts of love toward him already. I had never felt this kind of love before. I had never even laid eyes on him, yet I loved him dearly.

What I felt deep inside during the sonogram procedure was enlightening as well. A flood of emotions cascaded over me when we went to the doctor for the first sonogram and saw the image on the screen. I felt a deep love for this fetus. It simply was a fuzzy, black-and-white outline, yet I felt a deep love for this child. Yes, the attachment began very early for me.

With a subsequent sonogram we found out the gender of our child. Lisa wanted to know early the child's gender, but I wanted to wait and be surprised on the day of the birth. She was much more practical in her approach. Lisa did not want to paint the baby's room in neutral colors. Nor did she did want to receive infant clothes in neutral colors at our baby showers. She wanted to decorate the room appropriately and suggest clothing that would be gender-appropriate. She desired either blues or pinks and not greens and yellows.

When the attending nurse obtained on the screen a clear picture of our fetus, she asked, "Do you want to know what it is?" Lisa replied quickly, "Yes." Hesitantly, I agreed. "It's a boy," the nurse blurted. Of course, sonograms can be wrong, so Lisa inquired, "Are you sure?" "Yes, pretty sure," was the response. My wife quizzed, "How sure are you?" The nurse replied, "Well, if it's not a boy, I'll go to your home and repaint the walls of the baby's room for you."

Immediately, my mind raced. A son. Wow! God appeared to be giving us a son. I hadn't specifically prayed for a son, but now I felt such pride and joy since the odds were good that our baby would be a little boy. Right away I felt a connection with him. My love for him extended well-beyond his actual birth. It began much earlier. I'm not certain when and where it actually began, but that day in the examination room I certainly knew it was there.

Psalm 139 suddenly took on a more powerful meaning to me. In beautiful imagery the psalmist reflected, *For you created my inmost being. You knit me together in my mother's womb. I praise you because I am fearfully and wonderfully made. I know that full well. My frame was not hidden from you when I was made in the secret place. When I was woven together in the depths of the earth, you saw my unformed body* (Ps. 139:13-15). God's love connection with us extended far-beyond just our physical birth. His fatherly love was present even before we were formed. I felt the same love connection with Camden. I loved him while he was being formed and well before his actual birth. And God felt the same about me.

The intense feelings of love for our baby heightened as we heard the heartbeat and felt him kick in the womb. "This is interesting," I thought. I didn't even know my son and had never seen him. We weren't certain of his name. I only could try in my mind's eye to imagine what he would look like. Yet the love for him was apparent and powerful. Very early in Lisa's pregnancy it was present.

## LOVE IN THE BIRTHING ROOM

The first part of my son's body which I actually saw with my eyes was the top of his head. We were blessed to have a good friend and church member, Sherry Cook, working that evening as the nurse on duty at the hospital. She was very helpful in assisting with little Camden's entrance into this world. He only was about one hour away from his birth when

Sherry asked me, "Greg, would you like to see your son's head?" Through my weary eyes of hours without rest I saw the crown of his head. For the first time the love I felt for my son was realized into a person. Before, I had felt this strong emotion toward a fetus . . . something unseen. Now, I saw with my eyes a portion of his body. My heart was in my throat, my pulse quickened, and the love intensified.

When the moment arrived for Camden's entrance into the world, everything happened quickly. The gynecologist entered the room; the remainder of the event was a blur to me. Several nurses converged, so I faded into the background and allowed them to do their jobs. At 12:07 a.m. on July 4, 2003, our answered prayer arrived.

I have always heard parents speak of their first actions when their child was born. I heard them say that they counted fingers and toes and looked for deformities. Strangely, my desire was not to do that at all. From the moment he was born I felt true unconditional love for Camden. Whether he had any deformities or missing digits didn't seem that important. The fact was that he was my son and he was here!

One of the thoughts from the parable of the prodigal son (Luke 15) which strikes me the most is that the father did not need the son's confession when the young man returned home. The son rehearsed the speech and was intent on giving it. However no speech was necessary when the son returned. Words weren't important. The fact that the son was present was the greatest joy to the father. In some way I felt the same emotion when I was in the birthing room. Whether our baby was in perfect physical condition was not as important as was the fact he was here. And I loved him with all of my heart.

For years in Bible-study groups, discipleship classes, and my theological studies, I studied in the Bible about unconditional love. From every angle I had studied the topic in-depth.

And, from the perspective of a son, I had experienced it from my Heavenly Father. But five minutes after my son's birth, when I held Camden for the first time, I experienced unconditional love from the viewpoint of a father. It was a beautiful picture of love without any strings attached. Nothing could make me love my son more; nothing could make me love him less.

In the birthing room early on that holiday morning I breathed many prayers. I uttered prayers of thankfulness, direction, and wisdom. One of the prayers I spoke verbally was one of thankfulness for unconditional love. I was thankful that as a son, I had experienced such love from God. And I was thankful that now, as a father, I had experienced unconditional love. I had been uncertain whether I ever would get to experience this moment on this earth. But God was gracious to me and allowed me the privilege. Here I was, now a father—holding my son for the first time.

Yet as much love as I felt toward my son in those moments, God loves me even infinitely more than I love Camden. Early on that morning I was struck with this powerful realization as well. God's love truly is staggering. In this moment I felt it surround me. I wept.

### BEING OR DOING?

Christians often believe that God's love is predicated on their actions. Believers sometimes think that God loves them only because they love Him. God loves them because they are active in church. God loves them because they read their Bibles and are faithful to have a quiet time with Him. God loves them because they serve Him. Christians often believe that only when they are faithful does God love them.

However unconditional love means just that—it is without condition. Our Heavenly Father places no conditions on His love. Not one. God simply loves me because of who I am—His child. Unconditional love is based on being, not on doing. God's love is pure, uncontaminated love with no strings attached.

Camden is not always obedient to our commands. I wish he were, but he is not! Of course I suppose we are unrealistic to expect him to be perfect. From a parent's perspective his disobedience is often frustrating. (More about this later.) However my love for him doesn't change when he is disobedient. I do not love him less when he is defiant and do not love him more when he is compliant. My love for him does not change at all, regardless of his actions. I love him, period.

One of the primary doctrines for which we Southern Baptists are known as well as often criticized is the belief in the assurance of salvation. Southern Baptists have championed the phrase *once saved, always saved*. Critics argue that believers can fall from grace and lose their salvation. I believe in the assurance of salvation, not because I am a Southern Baptist minister, but because I believe Scripture teaches the doctrine. Jesus assured his disciples, *"And I give unto them eternal life and they shall never perish, neither shall any man pluck them out of my hand"* (John 10:28). In John 3:16 Jesus promised eternal life to anyone who believed in Him. His promise was that believers would not perish but would have everlasting life. Jesus could not promise me eternal life if my salvation is conditional. If I lost my salvation when I sinned, then I would have temporal life, not eternal life.

God's unconditional love is the reason we can be secure in our salvation. He does not discard us when we are disobedient. Does He desire for us to be disobedient? Of course not. Is He disappointed when we are disobedient? Sure, He is. But neither does He discard us nor disown us. Certainly I am disappointed when my son fails and is disobedient. I do not desire his disobedience. Yet nothing will make me discard him or disown him. He can do nothing to make me cease loving him or calling him my son. Unconditional love is not based on performance.

In similar fashion God knows we will fail. He remembers our humanity. The psalmist put things poignantly when he wrote, *As a father pities his children, so the Lord pities them that fear him. For he knows our frame; he remembers that we are dust* (Ps. 103:13-14). His desire is for perfect obedience to his commands, yet He knows our human nature will fail. I am certain that disobedience can be just as frustrating for our Heavenly Father as it is for earthly fathers. Yet we are comforted to know that God's love for us does not change depending on our obedience. He doesn't love us more when we obey His commands and reduce His love when we disobey.

From the very beginning one of the lessons we have tried to teach Camden is to pick up his toys when he is finished playing with them. It is a lesson he doesn't always grasp. I wish you could see our home at times! We tell him, "A part of having the privilege to play with your toys is to put them back in their places when you are through playing with them." We have repeated this phrase to him many, many times. For some reason, perhaps because I have repeated it so frequently, he dislikes putting his toys back into their places. He will do anything to get out of it. And for some reason—perhaps my personality trait of wanting everything in its place—I really feel irritated when his toys are scattered across the house, especially when I trip over them in a darkened room late at night. Yet in spite of how this trait annoys me and the extent to which he dislikes putting up his toys, my love for Camden does not change throughout the process.

God told his people repeatedly throughout their history that He is the Lord and that He does not change. The Israelites were obedient at times, yet more frequently they were disobedient. They did not learn their lessons from past failure and punishment. Time and again they repeated the same mistakes. Yet God's love, care, provision, and character were constant. He did not change. His love was not predicated on His children's actions. God's love was a result of being, not doing.

## LOVING WHAT HE LOVES

As Camden and I were driving to the church one day, he was watching on his portable DVD an episode of *Bob the Builder*. He was laughing and enjoying the animation. I said, "Boomer, I sure like *Bob the Builder*." He replied, "Me, too." I asked, "Do you know why I like *Bob the Builder* so much?" "Why?" he answered. "Because I like you and you like *Bob the Builder*."

Now, I must confess that before Camden was born, I did not enjoy watching animated cartoons or puppet shows. When I was a child, I enjoyed them, but years ago I stopped liking them. Yet for three years now for countless numbers of hours I have watched them faithfully. *Veggie Tales*, *Bob the Builder*, *Barney*, or *Sesame Street* would not be my choice if I were to choose a show to watch to relax for the evening. But there I am every night, watching one or all of them. In fact (please forget you read this and never remind me of it), I find myself looking forward to watching them. During the course of the day I quietly will think, "Just a few more hours and I get to watch *Elmo* and *Sesame Street*."

Why do I do this? The answer is very simple. Camden loves them. And I love him and desire to be with him. I do not love the animated cartoons and silly puppets, but I love the one who loves them. My perspective of them now is quite different. I love what he loves. There I am, just as enthralled as my son. He laughs and I laugh. He sings the songs and I sing the songs. He gestures the hand motions to the silly songs; I'll do the same. Now, during the course of the day, without my son anywhere near, I find myself humming or whistling one of these tunes. Funny how your perspective changes when you genuinely love.

When Camden began to enjoy certain things, I began to enjoy them. I love whatever he loves. I now find myself doing things that I would never have thought about. I find myself refraining from doing activities I thought I always would enjoy. Why? Only one word can explain it. *Love.* Not just an idle, passing, selfish love, but a pure, unconditional love from my heart.

I always have enjoyed sports tremendously. Whatever the season I always have enjoyed playing and watching that particular sport. Basketball, football, baseball. However my favorite sport while I was growing up was basketball. Before I totally committed my life to Jesus, basketball truly was my god. Each March I eagerly anticipate and thoroughly enjoy watching the NCAA Basketball Tournament on television. I complete my bracket of predictions and with delight watch each possession of March Madness.

In March 2005 Camden was just shy of his second birthday and at the height of his *Elmo* phase. This fuzzy *Sesame Street* character literally captivated his affection. One evening, Camden and I were lying on the bed watching an *Elmo* video together. Suddenly a thought hit me. "The Final Four basketball games are on!" Then, two questions raced through my mind. First, how did I forget something which for many, many years was such an integral part of my life? Second, why did I not have the desire to turn off the video (which we could watch any time) and tune in the games? Again, the best answer was love. Not a selfish, hedonistic kind of love, but a pure, unconditional love which I felt for my son. He loved watching the video; I loved him. Therefore I loved watching the video and did not want to watch the basketball game. That evening is sketched indelibly in my mind; I remember it fondly. Not because I missed a game but because I realized just how deeply I loved my son. I loved him far more than I did my own interests. I wanted to be involved in his interests. I'm certain God wants to be involved in my daily interests as well.

In my duties as a minister I am often called on to attend many functions and perform many activities. Honestly, some of them would not be my choice if I were simply choosing what I would want to do for the evening. I wish I could tell you that every time I leave my home to go on churchwide visitation that my motive for doing so is because lost people need to hear about Jesus. I wish I could say that every time I share my faith with someone, I do so because of my grave concern for his or her spiritual condition. But I would not be honest if I told you that on every single occasion that was the case. Many times I am motivated to visit and witness because of my love for people. But not always.

However I continue to perform these activities and as a minister have done so faithfully for more than 25 years. Why? Because I love the One who loves these people. *It is not God's will that any should perish, but all should come to repentance* (2 Pet. 3:9). Therefore I go and share. I set aside activities I would prefer doing because I love what God loves. Unconditional love can do nothing less.

# Chapter 3

# "I Don't Want to, but I Will"

One of my favorite stories is from the campaign trail of Gov. Christian Herter years ago. From 1953 to 1956 Herter served as the governor of Massachusetts and from 1959 to 1961 as United States Secretary of State. In 1961 the governor was seeking re-election to a second term in office and had been on the campaign trail all day. His busy schedule had taken him through many cities with numerous stops. Throughout the day he had eaten very little and eagerly awaited a fund-raising barbecue at a church in the evening.

When Herter finally arrived at the fundraiser, he was famished. The smell of fried chicken and mashed potatoes with gravy wafting through the air made him salivate. He went through the long line and anticipated the wonderful meal. The governor took his plate, silverware, and napkin and awaited the delicious food to be placed on his plate.

As he went through the line an elderly woman placed a single piece of chicken on his plate. The hungry governor paused and asked the frail woman, "Ma'am, may I please have another piece of chicken? I have been on the campaign trail all day and haven't had much to eat. I am famished. Would you please give me a second piece of chicken?" The woman replied, "Nope. Everybody gets one piece of chicken." Herter was somewhat surprised and miffed at her response. In desperation and frustration the governor asked her, "Ma'am, do you know who I am? I am the governor of this state!" The elderly woman replied, "And do you know who I am? I am the lady in charge of the chicken and everybody gets only one piece!"[1]

Christian Herter laughed and moved through the line but said he would never forget the incident. Here was a woman who was being obedient to the commands of a superior regardless of the status of one asking her to break the rules. If everyone was as obedient as was this frail, elderly woman at a Massachusetts fund-raiser, then our world would be a better place.

However being obedient is not that easy. Obedience is difficult for each of us. It is tough for any age group, especially for children. Time and time again a small child tries to assert his or her independence. The child has to decide who is in control and to what extent. Obedience is one of the first of many lessons he or she must learn.

Camden is still in the process of learning. He is trying to figure out how much of his life he controls and how much of it his parents control. Sometimes what goes on is a battle of the wills. But my son will learn what obedience looks like. And as he does so, I see a microcosm of my relationship with my Heavenly Father and what my obedience to Him looks like. How much of life will my little boy control and how much will I control? Likewise, in my relationship with my Heavenly Father, the same question applies. How much of my life will I attempt to control? How much of it am I allowing God to control?


## THE STORY OF THE PHRASE

We were amazed at how quickly a certain phrase emerged from my little boy's mouth. The phrase was: "I don't want

51

to!" Again and again we have heard this defiance. One moment he was learning to say heart-warming words such as *Mommy* and *Daddy*. The next moment he defiantly was saying, "But I don't want to!"

We feel as though our son rebels against almost any command we give him. "Camden, time to get ready for bed." "But, I don't want to." "Time for your bath." "But, I don't want to take a bath." "Son, pick up your toys." "But, I don't want to pick up my toys." "Time to leave the playground and go home." "But, I don't want to go home." The process seems endless. At times his disobedience makes us want to pull our hair out.

Where did he learn this? Is the desire to rebel against authority innate within every person? Did Adam and Eve demonstrate such defiance in the Garden of Eden? Are we born with a desire to go our own way? I was surprised and amazed at how early in life my son wanted to "do his own thing."

Of course at times we adults also want to utter the phrase, "I don't want to." Get up each day and go to work? Some days we simply want to say, "I don't want to." Use our hard-earned salary paying bills? Of course we don't want to. Have regular physical and dental exams? No, I don't want to. Change diapers at 3 a.m.? Well, you get the picture. But learning to do what you have to do despite your feelings of not wanting to is a natural part of maturing, growing, and becoming responsible.

At times spiritually we don't want to obey commands either. At times in our spiritual growth believers do not desire to be obedient to God. We may not want to attend church, tithe on our incomes, witness to a friend, study our Bibles, have a quiet time of devotion with God, or teach a Sunday-school class. What is the difference between my son's defiance and my disobedience to God's commands? Is the only difference that my son verbalizes his feelings and I do not? Again, my son's nature provided me with some valuable insight into my own selfish, sinful nature.

Does my desire to rebel against God's commands create the same feelings in my Heavenly Father as my son's disobedience creates in me? Does God become frustrated—even somewhat angry and develop an attitude of "I'll show you"?

After much discussion about Camden's phrase of disobedience, Lisa decided to try a new tactic, although I was skeptical. She sat down with our son one day and instructed him, "I understand that you have things you don't want to do. And I know that many times you don't want to obey a command we give you. But you have to obey when we tell you to do something. If you want to say, 'I don't want to,' then that's okay, but you still have to obey. From now on, say, 'I don't want to, but I will.'"

Well, surprisingly, it worked. We would issue a command; you could see the little wheels in his mind beginning to turn. "I don't want to, but I will." He reluctantly would carry out the command—all the time muttering and repeating, "I don't want to, but I will. I don't want to, but I will."

Later, when he grew a little older, we would tell Camden to do something. He would outright say again, "I don't want to." We would remind him of our previous conversation from months back and say, "Son, remember when you don't want to do something, you still must obey. Remember? 'I don't want to, but I will.'"

I'll admit it. I really didn't think that tactic would work. But it did and continues to work. And I'll also admit that many times in my relationship with my Heavenly Father, I really don't want to carry out one of His commands. Perhaps I'm tired or busy or simply selfishly want to do another activity. Now, whenever I find myself hesitant to obey God, my mind goes back to our conversation with our son. And from time to time, I find myself reluctantly obeying as I breathe a prayer, "Lord, I don't want to, but I will."


## MY OWN FATHER

My father was an interesting man. Lee Roy Ammons was an aggressive entrepreneur who had many vested interests. He was well-known in the southeastern Oklahoma region in which I was reared. For nearly 30 years he was a bank president but had other business ventures as well. My father owned an automobile dealership, a restaurant, and a farm-implement dealership, as well as other businesses. At one point he even built a plant to manufacture alternative fuel. He was a man very much ahead of his time. My father also led out in community and civic activities while he served as the mayor of our small town. He was busy, on-the-go, and energetic while in his 77 years of life accomplishing many feats.

I was very proud of my father. I felt privileged to be called his child and to bear his last name. When he was with me in public, especially if it were just my father and me, I was highly proud to be seen with him. I recall several specific instances in which I beamed inwardly as I was seen with him. When someone would say, "You must be Lee Roy's son," I would swell with pride.

However I always wanted to spend more time with my father and wish he would have spent more time with me. He loved me. I never doubted that fact. He provided for me and would have done anything for me. Yet I remember wanting desperately for him to arrive home early from the bank to play ball with me in the yard. I recall sitting in my yard and watching the highway. I hoped the next vehicle to travel down the hill would be my father's car. In my mind's eye I vividly remember leaning against a tree waiting for my dad to get home to take me to a Texas Rangers baseball game, which he had promised to do. I would look at my watch and calculate the latest time he could arrive home from work to enable us to still go to the game for the evening. Most of the time he arrived home too late and promised me that we would go to the ball game another night. If I could turn back the hands of time and magically change one feature of my relationship with my father, I would have spent more time with him.

When my Dad put his arm around me or I held his hand crossing the street, I felt like a million dollars! I felt totally safe from any harm whatsoever. I cannot describe this feeling but can still feel it to this day. I loved him, respected him, and was so very proud to be his son.

Because of my deep love for my father, I wanted to please him in every way. I never wanted to disappoint him. Therefore, my view of obedience as a child hinged on how I felt toward my father. To some degree I feared him. Not a physical, cringing fear, but a fear out of deep respect. When he told me to do something, I made sure that I did it. Disobedience to my father's command was not a part of my vocabulary. I obeyed out of respect for him even if I did not want to do so. Although I did not say, "I don't want to, but I will," I certainly acted on that principle.

My father died in January 2006 after a lengthy battle with cancer. I regret that my father's life and interests will never intersect with those of my son. Daddy wept the day we told our family that we were pregnant. He was very proud of us and rejoiced over the birth of our child. He loved Camden. Before he succumbed to his battle with cancer, Daddy was able to hold Camden and play with him in a limited way.

Unfortunately I don't recall events before about age 4 or possibly 5. What was my obedience to my father like when I was age 2 or 3? It probably was much like my son's obedience. The phrase "I don't want to" probably proceeded from my lips just as it does from my son now. At times as I interact with Camden, I still see my father. I see him in some of my actions as my little boy and I do things together. I still hear my father's voice as I listen to my words instructing my son. Although he was far from a perfect father, I loved my Dad and desired to please him in every way possible. I learned obedience to him which was predicated on my great love for him.

### OBEDIENCE IS LEARNED

One of the powerful scriptural principles I have learned from having a son is that obedience is learned. In fact obedience is not inherent in a human being at all. Precisely the opposite is true. Obedience is an acquired trait. We have a natural inclination toward disobedience. Something within the heart of every person pushes us toward disobedience. If you want to be obedient to God, to authorities, to the government, to parents, then remember that obedience is a learned behavior.

Notice how often in the Old Testament God placed His children in situations in which they were forced to learn obedience. Abraham was instructed to leave his family and kinsmen to journey to a land which flowed with milk and honey (Gen. 12). But at an older age he had to learn obedience in order to possess the blessings. Joseph had to learn obedience to God for his family to be saved during the famine (Gen. 37-50). Moses had to be obedient to God's commission before he could lead the Israelites (Ex. 2). Joshua commanded obedience from God's people before victory could be won (Josh. 24:15). Gideon learned obedience and reliance by being told to reduce his army before the powerful Midianites could be defeated (Judg. 6-8). David had to learn to obey before he could be a man after God's own heart (Acts. 13:22).

The Old Testament prophets spoke frequently about obedience. The Israelites were blessed when they obeyed; judgment fell on them when they were disobedient. Eighth-century prophets spoke of repentance and obedience being required if the Assyrian devastation was to be avoided. The Israelites were disobedient and failed to repent; therefore, the Assyrians captured the land. Later God's prophets warned the people of Judah of the same fate if they were unrepentant and disobedient. They continued in their sinful ways; the Babylonians pillaged their land. Joel spoke of the obedience required by God in the great Day of the Lord (Joel 2:11). Zechariah preached that obedience was required of God's people for the Temple to be rebuilt (Zech. 6:15).

In the New Testament God again placed His people in situations in which they had to learn obedience. Jesus repeatedly instructed His disciples in this manner. Time and again His followers saw the power of God displayed when they obeyed. The disciples learned valuable lessons of obedience, whether this involved trusting Jesus for food when a boy volunteered his lunch, casting their nets on the opposite side of the boat to catch fish, or failing to cast out demons because of a lack of prayer and fasting. Later both Peter and Paul learned obedience, spoke of obedience, practiced obedience, and in their New Testament letters wrote about obedience.

To me the most powerful passage of Scripture which teaches us that obedience is a learned behavior is found in Hebrews 5:8. The writer of Hebrews instructs us that even

Jesus, as a son, had to learn obedience. *Although he was a son, he learned obedience through what he suffered* (Heb. 5:8). If Jesus, in his humanity, had to learn obedience, we can be assured that we are to learn it as well.

Dr. B.J. Miller once said, "It is a great deal easier to do that which God gives us to do, no matter how difficult the task, rather than facing the consequences of disobedience."[2] As Christians we are to be obedient to God in all areas of life. What God desires of each of His children is unquestioned obedience regardless of the situation.

We live in a society of rules. To be a productive citizen in our society, I follow rules. Once I reached age 6, I submitted to the state's rule of mandatory education. I had to wait until I was 16 years of age before I could operate a motor vehicle on our highways. As an adult I'm expected to pay my taxes. I follow the rules of the road as I travel the highways, or else my privilege of driving could be revoked. As a citizen I'm to obey the city ordinances. Where did I learn this pattern of obedience which dominates my life today? I learned it as a young boy.

Today, if I am obstinate against commands to a higher authority in our society, then more than likely I will have difficulty submitting to the commands of God. Obedience is learned. I still am learning. God still places me in situations in which I have to learn to be obedient. Camden is still learning obedience. And, yes, at times obedience still is difficult for both of us.

## I WANT MY SON TO OBEY

I want Camden to be an obedient son. When we are in the privacy of our own home, I desire that he follow all of our commands. When we are in public, I want my son to obey us when we speak.

Why? Why do I want my son to obey me? Because of my own ego? Because I want Camden to know who's the boss? No, I want him to obey me because my commands to him are for his own good. Why do I want him to hold my hand as we cross the street? Because I want him to know I'm bigger and stronger than he is? No, because I know what the consequences could be if he isn't prudent in crossing the road.

In much the same way one of the reasons why God wants me to obey Him is because He knows far better than I do. He doesn't command my obedience just to show me that He is more powerful or that He is the boss. He knows what the consequences may be if I do not follow His commands exactly as He states.

Camden also has trouble realizing that my commands are for his good. Why is he required to eat vegetables or to clean his room? Why do I insist that he always wear shoes when we go somewhere in public? To a small child these commands seem silly and often unimportant. Yet we sometimes have the same trouble—realizing that God's commands actually are for our good. Why are we to be faithful to give 10 percent of our tithe back to the Lord? Why are we to be faithful to attend worship publicly each week? Why are believers to refrain from engaging in premarital sex or from living together outside of the bonds of marriage? To our culture these commands of God seem ridiculous. Yet each of them actually is for our own good.

How many of my commands do I want Camden to obey? That's a silly question to ask a parent, huh? Of course I want him to obey all of our commands every time. But, again, I return to the analogy of my relationship with my son and my relationship as a son to my Heavenly Father. How many of

His commands does God want me to obey? Again, a silly question, huh? Of course, He wants me to obey each of them. But do I obey them all? No. I seem to select certain commands that I believe He wants me to obey the most; the others are optional. I would never say that openly, but practically I seem to operate in that way.

Practically I know that Camden will not obey all of my commands. Yet that doesn't keep me from desiring that my son obey me perfectly. The standard is high. I want him to obey all of the time, although I know that he will not do so. God knows that I will not obey all of His commands. Yet that doesn't keep Him from desiring my perfect obedience. His standard is high. This realization actually changed the way I view my obedience to God. Again, for many years in the classroom I had studied obedience. But after my son was born, my personal obedience to God became a more personal concept to me.

I'm amazed at how quickly children pick up on which commands parents are adamant about their obeying and which commands they feel as if they can get by without following. Early on Camden knew not to wander into a street or parking lot without our supervision. And early on he also seemed to know that we wanted him to clean his room when we told him to do so, but he doesn't take that command as seriously as he does the previous command about crossing the road. Yet as a father I don't want my son to have selective obedience. I want him to take each of my commands seriously. Although he may place a higher priority on one command over another, I want him to obey each one I give him.

I'm equally amazed at how quickly God's children begin to "prioritize" the commands their Heavenly Father gives them. We seem to think we know which commands God really means and which ones are not as important to Him. We seem to think that refraining from murder and adultery or worshiping other gods are the big ones, like my street/parking lot command.

We also seem to think that commands to refrain from gluttony or to hold our tongue or the imperative to share our faith are lesser commands in God's eyes. Yet as our Father, God does not want us to have selective obedience. He doesn't want us to decide arbitrarily which command of His is the most important for us to obey. He views His commands to us through a different lens than do we. God wants His children to obey every command every time.

My son didn't take very long to begin asking, "Why?" when I gave him a command. And I would always tell him why his obedience to me was important, even when he was very young. I would say, "Son, you must always obey us when we tell you something. If you don't learn to obey us, then you will not learn to obey God." Camden's obedience to me, as his earthly father, is connected to how well he will obey God one day. This is the single greatest reason why I want my son to obey me. As an adult I want him to obey God to the letter, so early on I must teach him why obedience is vital.

## THE FRUSTRATION OF DEFIANCE

Many fairy tales conclude with the phrase "and they lived happily ever after." I easily could write this book from that perspective. We had been childless for many years and prayed for God to answer our prayer to have a child. He answered. We praised Him. God gave us a son later in life. Praise God; everything now is blissful! We all lived happily ever after. However, if I wrote from that perspective, I would not be truthful. On many days having a child is a tremendous challenge, despite the fact he was given to us miraculously.

Yesterday was one of those days. If you are a parent, you know what I am talking about—one of those days in which all is not bliss in child-rearing—one of those days in which your child seems to question every little detail. I don't want to romanticize our experience and make our story as if God's blessing of a son did not involve challenges. Most of the day Camden was defiant—over matters as simple as putting on his shoes. "But, I don't want to wear these shoes. But, I don't want to go to church. But, I don't want to eat supper. But, I don't want to go to bed. But, I don't want to . . .." You fill in the blank. Defiance is frustrating!

God understood the frustration of His children's defiance. On many occasions our Heavenly Father expressed frustration with the defiance of His creation. Remember the time in Genesis 6? God created humankind for fellowship. In Genesis 3 Adam and Eve made wrong choices in the Garden of Eden; sin entered our world. Only three chapters later humanity had grown so defiant that God was sorry He had created humankind. *And God saw that the wickedness of man was great in the earth and that every imagination of the thoughts of his heart was only evil continually. And it repented the Lord that he had made man on the earth, and it grieved him at his heart* (Gen. 6:5-6 KJV).

Remember the golden calf incident in Exodus 32? The Israelites grew impatient with both Moses and God. They believed the conversation between their God and their leader shouldn't be taking that long. They approached Aaron and said, "*Come, make us gods who will go before us. As for this fellow Moses who brought us up out of Egypt, we don't know what has happened to him*" (Ex. 32:1 KJV). So Aaron told the people to take off their golden earrings. He melted the gold and fashioned it into the form of a golden calf, which they worshiped. The people accepted these gods and bowed before them in homage.

On Mount Sinai, God told Moses to go down the mountain because His people had become corrupt. The Lord had been watching each of their actions and weighing each motive. He told Moses, *"I have seen these people and they are stiff-necked. Now, leave me alone so that my anger may burn against them and that I may destroy them. Then I will make you into a great nation"* (Ex. 32:10 KJV). God obviously was frustrated with the defiance of His people.

Remember when Jesus' disciples could not cast out a demon from an epileptic boy? All three synoptic gospels record this event in which a man from the crowd approached Jesus and begged the Savior to have mercy on him. The perplexed father told Jesus that the boy was suffering greatly as an epileptic. *"He often falls into the fire or into the water. I brought him to your disciples but they could not heal him"* (Mt. 17:16).

Jesus was frustrated with the disciples. He had trained and taught them, but they failed at a time when he most needed them. Jesus spoke to the disciples in frustration while he used a phrase somewhat out of character for Him, *"O unbelieving and perverse generation, how long shall I stay with you? How long shall I put up with you? Bring the boy here to me"* (Mt. 17:17). Of course we know that Jesus immediately healed the boy. Later the disciples wondered why they could not heal the youngster. Jesus further instructed them about prayer and fasting. Jesus Himself knew the frustration of His children's defiance.

Yesterday Camden was having a temper tantrum and was showing outright defiance to my command. He looked at me with tears streaming down his face, with fire in his eyes, and with a look of defiance in his gaze and said, "But, I don't want to!" I found myself in frustration thinking, "Oh, yes you will, young man!" Later, in the quietness of reflection on the event, God spoke in love to my spirit. It wasn't an audible voice I heard, but it was so clear that it could have been. "Greg, what you felt when your son was in outright defiance to your command is what I feel when you disobey Me. The frustration you felt is multiplied many times over when you defy My commands. Camden is only a child learning obedience. You have been my child for many years . . . you should know better by now."

My heart sank as I contemplated what I heard in my spirit. A gentle, loving Father had corrected me. I guess defiance is frustrating for anyone giving the command and expecting obedience. Here was yet another lesson learned from my boy about my relationship with God.


## MEDICINE TIME AND A SILLY FOOTBALL GAME

Infants and children seem constantly to contract colds and have runny noses. We keep the appropriate medicine on hand when Camden becomes severely congested. He especially loves one medication! It is grape-flavored, so most children would love it. However the second medication doesn't taste very good. It has a strong aftertaste and causes him to wince as he takes it. After each dose he makes an awful face and licks his lips for about 10 minutes afterward. Getting him to take the second medication always is a battle.

My son blessed me beyond measure on one congestive occasion when he was almost 2 years old. He gobbled down the grape-flavored medicine. Then arrived the time for battle over the dreaded, awful-tasting second medication. In preparation for the battle Lisa simply told Camden, "Honey, you need this medicine to make you feel better. I know it doesn't taste good, but take it for us."

With all of the strength his little 2-year-old body could muster, he set his jaw, gnarled his face, took a deep breath, opened his mouth, and gulped the medication. I was so proud of him! A lump developed in my throat as I realized that he did not want to take the medicine but did so simply because he knew we wanted him to take it. He was obedient when everything within him wanted to fight it. He simply trusted us.

Again my thoughts went spiraling toward heaven. Is God proud of me when I obey His commands even though I do not want to do so? I had never thought of how God felt when I obeyed simply to be obedient, although I had rather not do so. I confess that at times I am obedient to God, not because I want to do so, but simply because He has commanded it. I've already admitted that at times I go out on visitation, not out of a burning passion to see the lost saved, but simply because my Father has commanded me to go.

As I mentioned earlier, I am an avid Oklahoma Sooner fan. I was ecstatic when the Sooners played for the national championship of college football in 1985. At this time I was serving as the pastor of Floyd Baptist Church near Greenville. For weeks I had been anticipating the national championship game. As the day of the game neared, my anticipation grew. Each day I read the newspapers eagerly as the media hype about the game increased. The day of the game finally arrived. I was excited! I could hardly wait until the kickoff at 7 p.m.

At 6:45 p.m the telephone rang. An elderly, homebound woman in our community called and needed to counsel with me. She asked whether I could visit her. I hesitated answering her; in that split-second my mind began to race. I thought, "Lord, do I have to go? She isn't even a member of our church. She hasn't even attended our church once since I have been here. The Sooners may not play for another national championship in my lifetime. Her voice didn't appear to be overly distraught. Can't this wait until tomorrow? Lord, do I have to go?" Slowly I responded, "Sure, I'll be right there."

Like my son standing before me as I held the medicine dropper in my hand, I gulped, took my car keys, and headed for the door. I admit that I did not want to go. But simply out of obedience and for no other reason I drove to Greenville. I didn't get back until halftime of the game. However, to my elation, the Sooners beat Penn State and won the national championship.

As badly as defiance feels to a parent, a child's obedience brings that much joy. Emotions seem to be at opposite ends of the spectrum for parents when their child's obedience is concerned. I am so proud of Camden when he obeys! I am especially proud of him when I know that he really doesn't want to do something but does it simply to be obedient and for no other reason.

For more than 20 years I have remembered the football-game experience. In fact the telephone call and visit is more important in my mind now than is the game. It represents a time in which I was obedient when everything within me found reasons to be disobedient. I always want to bring joy to the heart of God. "God, I want to bring as much joy to You with my obedience as my little boy brought to me when he didn't want the medicine but took it. Father, may I always be an obedient child."

# Chapter 4

# God Is for Me

World War II was a difficult time worldwide. Country was divided against country. The Axis Powers, headlined by the "Big Three" of Nazi Germany, Japan, and Fascist Italy, attempted to control the world. Many other nations formed an alliance to fight the spread of the Axis Powers. On January 1, 1942, the Declaration of the United Nations officially united 26 nations in partnership to oppose the control of the Axis Powers. The "Big Three" of the Allied Nations were the United States, the United Kingdom, and the Soviet Union. Eventually, the allied efforts of these United Nations won World War II and halted the spread of the Axis Powers.[1] An ally has been defined as "one who cooperates with another toward a common purpose."[2] A great feat was accomplished worldwide through the allied efforts of these nations.

No one is in Camden's corner more than his parents are. We are on his side. We are for him. We desire the best for him. We are his allies. We are working together with him toward a common purpose. God has a specific plan for his life; we are working with him toward the goal of perfectly fulfilling this purpose. Of course, at his age now, he doesn't realize this wonderful fact, but it is still true. He doesn't realize how good life is for him and how much he is loved. He doesn't realize that his parents always will protect, love, care, and watch over him. He is always welcomed and wanted in our presence.

Christians are often unaware of all their Heavenly Father is to them and does for them. No one is in their corner more than God. He is for them. He is on their side. He truly desires the best for us. Yet as God's children, we do not often realize how good life is for us and how much we are loved. Our Heavenly Father always will protect, love, care, and watch over us. We are always welcomed and wanted in His presence.

## STANDING BESIDE OUR BED

Lisa and I awakened in the early hours of the morning. We had been asleep for quite some time, but now we awakened at almost the same time. You know the experience of being asleep yet seeming to have the gnawing feeling that someone is watching you? That was exactly how we felt on this morning. Almost with a keen sense of intuition, we awakened at almost exactly the same time and looked to our left.

Standing beside our bed was a shadowy figure. In the darkness of the room you sensed this presence more than you saw it. Someone definitely was standing beside our bed. Who was this person? Who would be brazen enough to walk into the privacy of our own bedroom and stand there looking at us while we slept?

If this person were a stranger whom we did not know, then this event would be a criminal act. It would violate our personal right to privacy. We would scramble for covers, panic, and begin asking this person questions. Without a moment's hesitation we would reach for the phone and call 911. Authorities would arrive to take this person away. A stranger is not welcome in our bedroom!

If this person were a friend, then this event would be curious. Close friendships are still not allowed access to your most private places and times. A close friend who would be brazen enough to walk into the privacy of our bedroom while we slept would be boorish. Although the act is not criminal, it would violate the bonds of a close friendship. To commit such an act a friend would be presumptuous at best and perhaps obnoxious.

But if this person were our son, we would have no cause for alarm. You see, he is welcome there. We would make no 911 phone calls. We would not scramble for cover. We would have no need to call authorities.We would have no need to speak with a close friend about the boundaries and parameters of our relationship. We would have no panic, because our son is welcome in our presence. He is welcome because he is one of us. He is ours.

Sure enough, the person standing beside our bed in the early-morning hours was Camden. And, no, we didn't panic. We simply looked at him; no words were exchanged. Lisa reached out to get him and placed him in bed beside us. We had no cause for alarm. This was no stranger. This was our son. He is welcomed in our most private setting in which no stranger or even close friend would be welcomed.

## ACCESS TO THE FATHER

John F. Kennedy served as the 35th President of the United States. Compared to previous couples who occupied the White House, both the President and First Lady, Jacqueline, were young. At a youthful 44 years old, Kennedy began his presidency and was rearing two children in the White House. Caroline was only 4 years old and John Junior (or John-John) was only 1 when their father assumed control of the most powerful nation in the free world.

John-John is said to have had the run of his father's office. The most trusted of advisors would enter Kennedy's office and find little John-John crawling under his father's desk while the President spoke on the telephone to world leaders. The young boy would be playing with cars and was oblivious to the fact that the most important person in the world was above him.

About a year into Kennedy's presidency, when John-John was almost 2, a photographer captured this powerful image. The poignant photo of John-John playing under his father's desk became a powerful image for our nation.

Was having access to the President's most intimate office an act of criminal intrusion? No, little John-John was welcomed in that setting. Other children would not have been allowed such entrance into such importance. But this was no ordinary boy. He was the son of the most powerful person in the world.[3]

One of the great blessings of being a child of God is that at any time, we are welcome in His presence. That was not always the case with God's children. Before Jesus died in our place as our sacrifice, the children of Israel could approach God only through a priest. On the Day of Atonement the Great High Priest would enter into the Holy of Holies on behalf of the people. He would offer an animal as a sacrifice for the sins of the people. Through this atoning sacrifice the people were made right with God.

Sins were atoned for, but the people still did not enjoy the freedom of walking in and out of God's presence. A veil hung as a reminder that a huge difference existed between a holy God and sinful humanity. The Outer Court, or Court of the People, was situated in the farthest point from the Holy of Holies. The veil hung as a visible reminder that God's children could not have instant access into His presence.

Then, on the cross, everything changed. At Calvary the way to God the Father was thrown open wide when Jesus died in our place. The Bible tells us that the veil of the Temple was torn from top to bottom. The visible reminder that God was not accessible to the people was removed. Did you notice that the veil was torn from top to bottom rather than from the bottom to the top? I believe even the tearing was symbolic. It shows us that the way to God was initiated by God (from top to bottom) rather than by humankind initiating the reconciliation (from bottom to top).

Now believers through faith in Jesus Christ at any time have immediate and unlimited access to God. Scripture tells us that through His blood we now have access to the Father. Like little John-John, we can make ourselves at home in the most powerful place in the universe right in the presence of the only God of heaven! Strangers to the covenant of promise do not have such access, but children do (Eph. 2:12). We are no ordinary children. We are children of the King!

Camden had access to our bedroom. John-John had access to the Oval Office. And, by faith in Jesus, you have access to the King of Kings.


## ADOPTED AS CHILDREN

A powerful image God uses to describe our relationship with Him is that of an adopted child. A child who is adopted is chosen because he or she is wanted. People who adopt certainly don't have a child by accident. An adoption only occurs when a child is desperately and deliberately wanted.

The Apostle Paul used the analogy of an adopted child almost exclusively to describe our standing with God. He told us plainly that God predestined us to be adopted as His children (Eph. 1:5). Have you ever considered this fact? Have you ever thought that God desperately and deliberately wanted you and chose you?

When someone is adopted, that child becomes an heir and enjoys family privileges. The New Testament is replete with passages in which believers are told they are heirs of all God possesses. Paul called believers heirs of God and joint heirs with Christ (Rom. 8:17). We are also told that believers are made heirs by God (Gal. 4:7), appointed heirs (Heb. 1:2), heirs of the gracious gift of salvation (1 Peter 3:7), and heirs of God's promises (Gal. 3:29). Scripture even tells us that Gentiles are also heirs by faith in Christ (Eph. 3:6).

Also, an adopted child usually receives the name of the adopting family. Accompanying the name are the rights and privileges associated with the name. Our Heavenly Father loved us so much that He gave us His name, *children of God*. Early believers first were called *Christians* in Antioch. Although it was a term of derision, the name meant "little Christ" and to believers became an endearing term.

On Camden's birth day no question ever arose that his last name would be Ammons. When we signed papers and told hospital authorities his name, people assumed that his last name would be Ammons. He was ours. Of course he would bear our name. He will forever bear our name, whether that name is good or bad. Camden will share any right or privilege because he has our last name.

What a great honor for Christians to bear the name of Christ! Of course, we bear His name—we are His! We are linked to Him forever. We share in all rights and privileges that accompany that wonderful Name! In Ephesians Paul told us that we are blessed with all spiritual blessings in heavenly places. What a blessing to be adopted as a child into God's family!

## WANDERING AWAY

Will God ever disown His children? Could we possibly wander so far away from Him that He no longer will be our Father? Sure, God may be for me when I first become His child. He is in my corner then. He is on my side at that time. But what about when I make wrong, sinful choices? Since He is holy and perfect, doesn't He disown me when I sin? How can I truly bear the name of a holy God while I continually make wrong choices? Will I truly be a child of God forever, or will my sinfulness exclude me from His family?

Theological debates still rage over these questions. Many belief systems hold that once you sin, you are excluded from God's family and no longer are His child. They contend that you must become a Christian all over again. However the Bible teaches that you can be secure in your relationship with God. If you are truly a child of God, then you will always be His child. He will never leave nor forsake you.

The most obvious passage of Scripture establishing this fact is John 3:16. In this powerful verse Jesus promised that whoever believes in Him will not perish but will have everlasting life. If I can be a child of God by faith in Jesus but make a wrong, sinful choice and lose my salvation, then what I possessed was not "eternal" life. I simply possessed "temporary" life. I held it as long as I was perfect but lost it the moment I sinned. Jesus promised eternal life and not temporary life.

Also the apostle Paul made it clear that our salvation is not works-based but is faith-based (Eph. 2:8-9). He stated that we are saved by grace through faith and not of works. If I did not work my way into salvation, then how can I work my way out of salvation? If I did nothing to earn a relationship with God, then how can my sinful actions take that relationship away? Salvation is a work of God, not a work of mine.

A time will never exist when Camden is no longer my son. A time won't occur when I do not love him. At times he will fail and disappoint me terribly. In fact many times he already has! Yet his failure does not sever our relationship. He will always be my son. It is a biological fact; nothing will remove the biological fact that he is my son. He could even deny the fact or I could deny the fact, but our denial does not remove the biological fact. Camden is my son and always will be my son.

Although our relationship does not change, our fellowship may change. His sinful actions may cause our fellowship to be severed. The biological fact of sonship is not altered, yet walking in close fellowship with each other may change with circumstances. Actions could cause our relationship to be strained, but Camden remains my child. My sinful actions cause my fellowship with God to be strained or severed, but I remain a child of His. I make sure that I seek His forgiveness and remain in fellowship with God, but I need never worry that my relationship will be forfeited.

In Luke 15 Jesus spoke three powerful parables of "lost-ness". The third of these parables drives home the point of fellowship without losing sonship. You may remember the story. A son wanted his father's inheritance and sought to distance himself from his dad. Legally the father could grant this request but didn't have to do so. The father, giving the son complete freedom, distributed the inheritance; the boy left home. Once on his own the son spent the inheritance freely and wasted it away.

Soon a famine hit the land; the son began to be in want. He had no money left yet was hungry and forced to search for a job. His desperate condition was revealed by the type of job he accepted—feeding pigs. Nothing is wrong with feeding pigs . . . unless you were a Jew in the first century. The Old

Testament law forbade Jews from touching swine (Deut. 14:8) The son was so desperate that he fed pigs and even envied the pigs as they ate.

Finally the young man came to his senses and asked himself a question. "What am I doing here? When I was home with my father, I had everything at my disposal. But now, here I am, feeding swine; they are eating better than me! My father's hired servants live better than me." He decided that he would return home and simply try to secure a job as his father's servant.

The anxious father had been watching for the son to return home. Finally one day he saw his son walking down the road. The father ran toward the son and grabbed him and kissed him. The son began to make an impassioned plea to be accepted merely as a servant. But the father interrupted and called for a ring for his finger, a robe for his back, and sandals for his feet. In that culture a ring symbolized authority, while a robe and sandals indicated sonship. Servants enjoyed none of these, but sons did. The fatted calf was killed; a party ensued because the lost son had returned home.

This is a revealing story about our relationship with God. The son did not lose his sonship. The father did not regard the boy as an "ex-son" who needed to earn his way back into sonship. The fellowship with the father was severed and needed restoration, but the sonship remained, even when the boy was in a far country.

Camden has wandered away from fellowship with me and will do so, I'm sure, many more times in our lifetime. Yet he always will be my son. I am thankful that my wandering away from God doesn't sever my relationship with Him. I make great effort to walk with my Heavenly Father in fellowship each day. But, I can rest secure in my sonship. His grace is sufficient for me.

When I interviewed the ministers for this book, several questions centered on how these ministers, once they became fathers, viewed God's attributes. I asked, "After you became a father, which attribute of God became most close to you?" The most frequent answer related to God's grace. These ministers understood more clearly, once they became fathers, that God's favor truly is unmerited. Their children often failed, yet those children were not disowned. As God's children we often wander away, yet grace will never let us go.

### BEING PROUD OF MY SON

Just as he approached age 3 Camden began to love superheroes. Batman. Superman. Spiderman. Power Rangers. Frogman. He loved them all. And he wanted to have all of the memorabilia of each superhero. (Marketers know what they are doing!) He went through a phase in which he wanted to wear the costumes of various superheroes when we went out into the public.

Yesterday Camden and I went to the post office and supermarket. He insisted that the day was Superman Day. He carefully retrieved all of his Superman gear for me to put it on him just so we could go to the post office and grocery store. One by one I put each item on him—the underwear, shirt, cape, shorts, socks, and shoes all consisted of his Superman outfit. He even insisted I comb his hair like Superman combed his hair.

As we walked into the post office, was I embarrassed to be seen with a little boy looking like this? Of course not! I thought he was cute. No one else may have thought so, but I did. I watched as people noticed my little boy and waited for their reactions. I loved these moments. I walked with pride while I held the little hand of my little Superman. We had a great time.

I cannot begin to tell you how proud I am of my son. Have you detected this fact throughout the pages of this book? I do not mean to imply pride in a sinful way, as Scripture warns against. I am speaking of a pride that wells up within me and stems from a simple relationship with my boy. No, he isn't perfect. Yes, he makes mistakes. No, he will never fulfill all I have dreamed for him. But I love him dearly and am so proud of him! Of course I want him to behave well, but I am proud of him regardless.

Before I had a son of my own, I had never thought about God being proud of me. God? Proud of me? I had never considered the thought. I knew God loved me. I knew God forgave me. I knew God considered me His child through faith in Jesus Christ. I knew God had a plan for me. I knew God had called me into His vocational service. I knew God was patient with me. But was God proud of me? Simply because I was His child?

Slowly I began to notice instances in Scripture in which God seemed proud of His children. If you read carefully, you can find the passages. The Bible never actually uses the phrase, "God is proud of His children." But the concept certainly is there.

Remember Job's story and the title of this book? In Job 1 Satan appeared before God in a heavenly council in which God initiated the conversation with the evil one about Job. *"Have you considered my servant Job? There is no one on earth like him. He is blameless and upright, a man who fears God and shuns evil"* (Job 1:8). God seemed to be a proud father. In the Lord's voice you can detect how proud He was of His child. He was proud of the way Job served and how he was blameless and upright. God seemed to beam as He spoke of how Job feared Him and refused evil. God declared no one was like Job. He was almost bragging on His child.

Was Job perfect? No. He had faults and failures. But God was still proud of him. Is Camden perfect? Certainly not. He fails each day. Are you perfect? Of course not. Each day we all sin.

Yet know today that if you are a believer in Jesus, God is on your side. He considers you His child. You will always be His child. He loves you and promises to forgive you. He is . . . well . . . proud of you.


## BEING ANGRY WITH HIM

OK, I confess. In the Ammons home everything is not rosy all of the time. Just because I recognize that Camden is a miraculous child given to us later in life doesn't mean I never become agitated. At times he frustrates me. At times I become angry with him. At times as a parent I get discouraged. Yet I never have a time in which I regret having him. Ever.

Now I understand why Paul offered advice to parents about their parenting skills. I see more clearly why the great apostle wrote to the churches of Ephesus, *Fathers, do not exasperate your children. Instead, bring them up in the training and instruction of the Lord* (Eph. 6:4). Paul's instruction to the church at Colossae, when he implored, *Fathers, do not embitter your children or they will become discouraged* (Col. 3:21) now makes more sense to me.

I am not angry when he makes honest mistakes, because he is simply too young to understand much. I do not become enraged when he spills a drink or drops food on the carpet. These accidents happen with children. However I grow angry with my son when he deliberately disobeys. The most frustrating moments are the times in which I have told him repeatedly and he knows better but simply chooses to be disobedient. These are the moments that test my patience.

On several occasions Scripture tells us that our loving, Heavenly Father became angry with His children. During the golden calf incident, which I described in Chapter 3, God told Moses about the Israelites, "*Let Me alone so My anger may burn against them*" (Ex. 32:10). The Lord was angered when His children failed to trust Him for Canaan at Kadesh-Barnea and refused to enter the Promised Land (Num. 32:10). When the Book of the Law was found by Hilkiah and King Josiah commanded it be read before the people, the Israelites discovered that God's anger burned against their forefathers because of their disobedience (2 Kings 22:13).

The times in which God's anger was aroused against His people the greatest were those moments in which they deliberately disobeyed. He was not angered by their accidents or unknowing mistakes. During the times when His people chose willingly to disobey and distrust, God became angry. When I discovered this fact about my Heavenly Father and about myself, I understood better which actions of mine angered the Lord and which pleased Him.

I simply cannot stay angry with Camden despite how frustrated I become with him. Yes, I become angry for a moment and frustrated for a short season, but my steadfast love for him does not allow me to hold my anger. I simply cannot do so. I find that pure love overcomes my frustration.

As I read Scripture, I began to understand that God's unconditional love for us overrides His anger. In his beautiful prayer of Numbers 14 Moses reminded the Lord that He punished disobedience yet still is *slow to anger, abounding in love and forgiving of sin and rebellion* (Num. 14:18). On three separate occasions (Ps. 30:5; 86:15; 103:8) the psalmists portrayed God as *slow to anger and abounding in love*. God may be angered for a season, but our repentance brings His favor.

## GIVING MY SON GIFTS

Since Camden was born, I find myself doing things that I had never done before. In fact, in a million years I would have never guessed that I would have done some of the activities I find myself doing now! In the last three years I have eaten at McDonald's more than I did in my first 43 years of life combined before Camden entered our home. Until three years ago I never even knew what a Happy Meal was.

Quite honestly, one day at McDonald's I did something of which I am not proud, but I guess confession is good for the soul. I hate to admit this, but I ate at McDonald's by myself one day at lunch and ordered a Happy Meal just for the toy car inside. You see, my son was collecting a set of cars given away in Happy Meal promotions. Except for two cars he had the complete set. One day while I was at the church office, I did not have a lunch appointment with anyone, so I went to a nearby McDonald's and ordered a Happy Meal. I was excited when it arrived and wondered which car would be inside. I was hoping to get one of the two which Camden did not possess. The hamburger and fries with the meal were afterthoughts.

Why would a grown man do this? Because I really enjoy giving my son gifts. I love to watch his little face light up when he sees a gift I've brought him. Before I had a child, I had no idea what pleasure I would get from giving gifts to my son. I know Jesus said giving is better than receiving; I have experienced joy in giving before. But I had never known such pleasure in giving a gift to another human being like I enjoy giving gifts to my son. In fact, I think I get more excited about the gifts than he does.

Lisa and I enjoyed an Alaskan cruise when Camden was only 8-months old. I was leading the cruise with several members of Faith Baptist Church of Iowa Park, where I served as pastor. We were gone for eight days. Being gone for that length of time away from our baby was heart-wrenching. While on the cruise we stopped at several ports of call and visited many sights with wonderful souvenir shops. In each shop we entered and browsed, I saw Camden.

At each stop I wanted to buy him a gift to bring back to him. The more days that passed, the more gifts I wanted to buy him! No expense was too great. I wanted him to have gifts and to know that we missed him and loved him very much. Fortunately for our pocketbooks, I exercised self-restraint and bought him only a few gifts. I could hardly wait to get back to Seattle, where Camden was staying with Lisa's sister, to give him the gifts we had purchased. They were small, monetary ways to show him our great love for him.

What Jesus spoke in the Sermon on the Mount made much more sense to me after our Alaskan vacation. If you remember, Jesus was speaking about prayer and how we are to ask, seek, and knock. He said everyone who asks receives, he who seeks finds, and to him who knocks, the door will be opened (Mt. 7:8).

The following part which Jesus spoke has really sprung alive for me now. *"Which of you, if his son asks for bread, will give him a stone? Or if he asks for a fish, will give him a snake? If you, then, though you are evil, know how to give good gifts to your children, how much more will your Father in heaven give good gifts to those who ask him?"* (Mt. 7:9-11) As much as I love giving good gifts to Camden, my Heavenly Father loves giving good gifts to me even more!

Many Christians have the image of a God in heaven who is stingy and reluctant to give. Often believers view God as an ogre who gives reluctantly after we have pleaded and begged. But Scripture paints a different portrait of a gracious, loving God who loves to give gifts to His children. In fact James said that every good and perfect gift is from our Father above (Jas. 1:17).

My newfound love of gift-giving made me stop and analyze what kind of good gifts God has given me. He has given me health, a sound mind, and the ability to think and reason. He has given me clothing, shelter, food, and all of life's necessities. He allowed me to be born in a region of the world in which His Son, Jesus, is openly preached and taught.

Then, of course, God's greatest gift to me is the gift of Jesus Himself. The Apostle Paul felt the same gratitude as he thanked God for his indescribable gift (2 Cor. 9:15). Earlier he had described salvation as a gift of God (Eph. 2:8). After salvation God gave me the gift of the Holy Spirit (Acts 2:38). Then God gave me spiritual gifts which would empower me to serve Him (Eph. 4:8).

God desires to give me—His child—His best gifts, much like I wanted to purchase good gifts for my son while I was in Alaska. Fortunately for me, He did not exercise restraint. He lavished me with the most expensive gift of all—His Son, Jesus, on the cross.

I love Camden dearly and love giving him gifts, but I have never given him gifts more precious than those given to me by my Heavenly Father. I certainly thank God, as did the Apostle Paul, for His indescribable gift.

## DESIRING HIS BEST

I want the very best for my son. I want him to have the best life possible. I want him to have the best spiritual instruction, the best home life, the best friends, the best education, and the best training possible. To help facilitate this goal I want to be the best father possible. Lisa is a wonderful mother. My son certainly has the best maternal care. I love him so much that I want the very best for him.

Interestingly, as we push Camden to be his best, even at a young age he seeks our approval. On one occasion just before he turned 3, Lisa and I were at a playground with our son. He was climbing through a plastic maze of toys. At the very top was a tunnel with a window from the perch down to the ground. Camden had made his way up through the tunnel to the top; he was quite proud of himself. He also knew that we would be quite proud of him as well. So when he reached the pinnacle of the jungle-gym world, he looked down and screamed at us, "Mommy! Daddy! Look at me!" Of course he was screaming loud enough for all of Dallas County to hear. Other parents and children stopped what they were doing to watch him. Along with the screaming he was so proud of himself that he was jumping up and down excitedly. To be perfectly honest with you, he looked rather awkward and goofy. But did we tell him how he looked? No, sir. Did we chastise him for embarrassing us in public? No way. We applauded and praised and raved about his wonderful accomplishment. In fact, at that moment, I didn't care publicly how I looked to others, nor did he. He desired our cheers. We wanted our son to know that he had our full approval. With me, he had an audience of one.

Does God desire our very best? I believe He does. Perhaps what I feel as a father desiring my son's best is akin to what

Jesus meant when He stated in John 10:10, "*I have come that they may have life and have it more abundantly* (KJV)." Exactly what did Jesus mean by an abundant life? One version translates *abundant* as "living life to the fullest." This is what I want for my son . . . that he live life to the fullest. God desires that I have the very best and be my very best. And, yes, at times we desire His approval. Our Heavenly Father lets us know how proud He is of us regardless of how awkward or uncomfortable we may appear.

Many people view God as someone who is against them. They picture Him in heaven with a lightning bolt in each hand and thunder in His voice. They believe that the Lord is waiting to cast the bolts and thunder in anger against them as soon as they fail to measure up to His standard or they simply make a mistake. However Scripture portrays a loving Father who truly desires the best for His child. God really is for you. He truly is in your corner. He really is on your side. With Him, you have an audience of One.

# Chapter 5

# Spending Time with My Son

During the Nixon and Ford Presidential administrations *Henry Kissinger* became a household name in United States history. During this time the German-born American diplomat served both as the U.S. Security Advisor and Secretary of State. From 1969-1977 Kissinger played a dominant role in our nation's foreign policy. He even is credited with easing tension between the United States and the Soviet Union during a time period in which hostility was high. Leaders worldwide recognized his brilliance and wisdom.

After such an influential career Kissinger reflected with an interviewer on his accomplishments. The host asked Kissinger what surprised him the most about his brilliant political life. Was it his importance in the Soviet Union deliberations? Or was he surprised at the amount of influence he wielded in East Timor with African policy? After moments of careful contemplation Kissinger replied, "What has most surprised me about my service in this country is how quickly it all passed."[1]

Since Camden's birth many people have advised me to enjoy each moment with my son. "It will pass so quickly, you will wonder where the time has gone," people often say. I realize this fact and want to make the most of each moment with him. Being an older first-time father has made me much more aware of life's brevity and to value each passing day. I want each day to count, especially when I am with my family.

I really enjoy Fridays. In general Friday is my day out of the office each week. Occasionally I will have to work, perform a funeral, or do some other church-related activity, but for the most part, each Friday is my day off. I really enjoy this day because I get to spend time with my family.

Each Friday when Camden awakens, we turn on the television and search for cartoons. He loves cartoons. We lie in bed together and watch his favorites—*Little Bear, Franklin, Dora the Explorer, Diego*. I'll watch with him and comment on what is happening. Often I will watch him as much as I watch the cartoon. I'll laugh just to watch him laugh. It's a special time—not so much because I really enjoy the cartoons; I just enjoy spending time with my son.

Writing this book is a wonderful experience for me because I have the opportunity to pen my thoughts about how much I have learned about God from my son. However even this experience is bittersweet for me, since the discipline of writing often takes time away from Camden. Usually I write very early in the morning before he awakens, so I don t lose precious time with him. I would rather lose sleep personally than lose time with Camden.

### THE JOY OF THE MOMENT

Why do I eagerly anticipate watching cartoons, which I haven't done in 40 years? Very simple—I really enjoy the time in which I can be by my son's side and participate in what he enjoys. I enjoy lying beside him, glancing over at him, and noticing the intensity on his face as he enjoys the cartoon. He really gets into them! Occasionally I'll throw in an exclamation just to watch his intensity increase. "Wow, son, did you see that?" "YES!" he will exclaim. I love being around him, doing things with him, sharing life together with him, and being involved in all of his activities and interests.

One of the most powerful lessons I learned from my son was how much God wants to spend time with me. Never before had I viewed my daily devotional time from His perspective.

At age 9 I became a Christian. I was in a Sunday-morning worship service at the First Baptist Church of Boswell, OK. During the invitation I walked to the front of the church and accepted Jesus Christ as my personal Savior and Lord. It was a special time; with the faith of a 9-year-old boy, I trusted Jesus. However only when I was 19 years old did I truly begin to grow as a believer. In the early 1970s discipleship wasn't emphasized as much as evangelism was. Often new converts would be baptized and then left to fend for themselves in the area of spiritual growth.

During the summer of 1979 I rededicated my life to the Lord and surrendered to God's calling on my life into vocational ministry. At this time my pastor, Larry Stevenson, sat down with me and taught me about discipleship. Our group met each Sunday evening after the worship service. Nine other teens, including my future wife, met with my pastor and me as we studied material about how to grow as a disciple of Jesus.

Throughout that wonderful summer I learned much about my Heavenly Father. I learned how to have a daily devotional time with God. I learned the discipline of such a vital time in my walk with Christ and in pleasing Him. So I began the practice of a daily Quiet Time with my Heavenly Father. For 27 years now I have enjoyed such times. But I always had viewed my devotional time as something important for me. I knew that I needed to have my devotional time with God for my growth, my development, my power, and my daily living, but the emphasis always was on the word *my*. Quite frankly, until I had a son of my own, I had never viewed my devotional time each day from the perspective of God.

The cartoon time each Friday morning shed an entirely new light on my Quiet Time. God truly enjoys spending time with me—His child—just as I thoroughly enjoy spending time with my son. God loves me much, much more than I love my son. He desires those moments with me. He enjoys being involved in my activities and interests. I wonder whether God loves to watch me, as I go through life, just as I love watching my son enjoy his cartoon shows. I wonder if my Heavenly Father throws in an occasional exclamation just to watch my intensity increase. "Enjoy this sunset, Greg." "Did you like the beautiful rainbow I stretched across your backyard last month?" I am sure God loves to watch as I enjoy life.

## GOD WALKED WITH HIS PEOPLE

As I began to realize how much I enjoyed spending time with my son and made the correlation to my spending time with God, I began to think about passages in Scripture in which God fellowshiped with His people. Most of the passages include the phrase *walking*. In biblical times to *walk* with someone was to share a special, fellowship time with that person. God loved to walk with His people.

These special moments when God walked with His children began early in Scripture. In Genesis 3 God walked with His new creations, Adam and Eve, in the cool of the day. They walked together in this special time until sin separated their fellowship.

Genesis 5:24 tells us that Enoch walked with God. Throughout the years this verse has meant much to me and became even more enlightening after my son was born. In this wonderful passage Scripture tells us, *Enoch walked with God. Then he was no more, because God took him away.* Some commentators over the years have viewed this passage as God having pity on an old man and simply taking him on home to glory. Yet if you read the passage carefully, this verse appears in the context of a genealogy. Enoch was not an old man whom God pitied and took home to heaven. He was about one-half the age of his contemporaries in the chapter. Evidently Enoch had a wonderful fellowship time with God. Our Heavenly Father valued this. One theologian paraphrased the conversation by stating that perhaps God said, "Enoch, I enjoy our walking together. The day is getting late; you are closer to My home than yours. Why don't you simply come home with Me?" Enoch was only one of two men in Scripture who never died; God simply took them home.

Later, as He gave them the Levitical laws, God told His people, *"I will walk among you and be Your God"* (Lev. 26:12). Moses commanded the people to walk in all of God's ways and to love Him with all of their hearts (Deut. 10:12). Joshua commanded the Israelites to do the same when he succeeded Moses (Josh. 22:5). The prophet Isaiah reminded God's people that they were to walk in His paths and in the light of the Lord (Isa. 2:2, 5). In the eighth century the prophet Amos commanded the people to repent and return to the Lord. *"Can two walk together unless they agree?"* he asked (Amos 3:3). In the book of Micah the Israelites wondered what they were to do to please God. The prophet responded, *"Love mercy, do justice and walk humbly with your God"* (Mic. 6:8). In the New Testament John told believers that if they had fellowship with the Father, they would not walk in darkness but would walk in the light (1 John 1:6-7).

Many things amaze me about Jesus. As I read about His life and reflect on how He ministered, I find the Son of God simply amazing. I enjoy dissecting what He did and why He did it. One of the most enlightening facts about Jesus is how He spent time with the Father. Before He chose His disciples, He prayed all night. He sent His followers away so He could be alone in prayer with the Father (Mark 6:46). Judas knew where to direct the authorities to find Jesus and to arrest Him—the Garden of Gethsemane, where the Betrayer knew Jesus would be spending time with the Father. If anyone ever existed who did not need to spend time with God in prayer, Jesus qualified. Yet He retreated for protracted times alone with the Father. If Jesus needed such a vital time with the Father, then I certainly need such a time.

God desperately wants to spend time with His people. Yes, a daily devotional time benefits me. It strengthens me for the day, teaches me His Word, allows me to grow in my faith, and develops discipline. But more important than the benefits I receive is the fact that my Heavenly Father loves me and desires to walk with me. Yes, Camden's arrival gave me a new perspective. Now, I view the time from God's perspective as well as from that of a son.

## HAVE I TOLD YOU LATELY?

My guess is that any parent absolutely loves to hear three little words. A parent may have no better moment than when his or her child says "I love you." Many children say these three powerful words simply to ease the punishment of any trouble into which they may have wandered. Parents can see through that scheme. However, when children honestly mean it when they say it, the moment is magical.

I remember the first time, unprompted, that Camden told me he loved me. We were going through the evening routine of bath time, putting on the night clothes, drinking juice, reading a book or telling a story, and turning out the lights. The night was merely average and ordinary. In the middle of the routine my son looked up at me and said, "I love you, Daddy." I can't describe the warmth that my heart felt. In fact, it melted. Of course I quickly said, "I love you, too, son. I love you very much."

When I was being reared, I wasn't told very frequently that I was loved. Oh, my parents loved me. In fact, they loved me dearly. In a myriad of ways they showed their love for me. I always felt loved, secure, and cared for by wonderful parents. However they didn't often state their love to me verbally. To have my child say "I love you" simply melted my heart.

Since then I have probably gone overboard with telling my son I love him. Perhaps I did this because I missed hearing these words when I was a child. I tell him constantly that I love him. Maybe after he hears it so frequently, this powerful fact is getting through to him. Once Camden was staying with friends for a few days. They had gone to see a movie and were on the way back home when one of the family members said, "Boomer, did you know that we love you?" His response was, "I miss my Mommy and Daddy." Hopefully, the sound of the wonderful words *I love you* made him think of home.

Now, Camden always tells me that he loves me when I am out of town or away from home for the evening and call back to speak to my family. Each time he tells me, it is a very special time for me. I never tire of hearing it. Those three words always bless my heart.

When my son first told me that he loved me, I again reflected on my relationship with God. Does God feel the same each time I tell Him that I love Him? When I say, "God, I love you," does my Heavenly Father's heart melt with joy? When we speak of God's feelings, I know that we use anthropomorphic language to describe Him, because He is a Spirit. But He is the One who used the analogy of a father and son to describe His relationship to us. So the comparison of the two is valid. What are His feelings when I tell God how much I love Him?

I believe that He experiences joy, just as I experience it. Perhaps I don't tell my Heavenly Father enough how much He means to me. Perhaps I am too busy going through a laundry list of needs and all of the ways I want Him to help me to say those three powerful words. Or perhaps I am too focused on all of the things I want Him to do for me and forget to tell Him that I love Him. I would experience a wonderful time in prayer just telling God how much I love Him.

I don't mind Camden asking me for things he wants. In fact I am delighted to get something for Him which He needs. So I don't mind his asking. However that moment in which he told me that he loved me from a genuine heart brought such joy to me that I cannot describe it. I feel tremendous love for my Heavenly Father. I plan to tell Him those three magical words more often.

I always have enjoyed the beautiful lyrics of a song written by Van Morrison and recorded by Rod Stewart. I prefer Christian music over secular music, but the first time I heard them, the lyrics of this secular song were special to me. In fact it later was recorded again as a Christian song. The song is entitled, "Have I Told You Lately?"

"Have I told you lately that I love you?
    Have I told you there's no one else above you?
You fill my heart with gladness, take away all my sadness,
    You ease my troubles, that's what you do.

"There's a love less defined,
And it's yours and its mine,
And at the end of the day,
    We should give thanks and pray
To the One, To the One.

"Have I told you lately that I love you?"[2]

Three little words, but they mean so very much. From the lips of a small child they blessed the heart of this father. And they will bless the heart of my Heavenly Father each time I say them from a genuine heart. Hopefully when you hear the words *I love you*, you, too, will think of home.

### HIS INTERESTS ARE MY INTERESTS

Lisa was scheduled to attend a weekend women's retreat with our church. It was held at a nearby hotel in Dallas. Camden was 2 years old; I was to take care of him for the weekend. Camden and I both were geared up and excited for the time together. In fact we had made big plans.

Boomer and I drove Lisa to the hotel for the retreat. We all were excited about the weekend ahead. I helped Lisa with her suitcase and travel bag; we all said goodbye, and Camden and I drove off. An awkward silence prevailed for a few blocks as we left the hotel parking lot. Finally I turned around to look at my son in the car seat. He sat there with huge tears rolling down his little cheeks. Then, all of a sudden as if the dam burst, he began to scream, "I want my mommy!" Oh, boy! Was this how the entire weekend was going to be?

I finally calmed my little boy down with promises of what we would do for the next couple of days. We ate at McDonald's and played on the playground, went to the park, played soccer, played golf, played basketball, ran races, ate ice cream—you name it; we did it. Everything he wanted to do, I joined in with him. Every interest of his was an interest of mine. He didn't cry for his mother any more. We were too absorbed in what he wanted to do.

The weekend was great. We had a blast! I wouldn't trade that special time for anything. It was extremely tiring and exhausting. I certainly understand what my wife goes through each day while I am at the church office. But it was one of the most memorable weekends I have spent.

Why was I keenly interested in what my son wanted to do for the weekend? Because I love him. I would not have chosen the same activities if I simply were home alone for the weekend with my wife away at a retreat. But if you truly love, then you share interests.

Again I could not help but think about my relationship with God and sharing His interests. Becoming selfish and self-absorbed in the Christian life is so easy. My interests, hobbies, and activities become my sole obsession. If I truly love God, then why are His interests not my interests? What are His interests? Well, Scripture defines them clearly. Advancing the kingdom of God. Bringing the lost into a saving relationship with Jesus Christ. Meeting needs in His name. Why do these activities not consume more of my time, just as my son's interests command my attention?

In the 1940s Russian-born novelist Vladimir Nabokov and his family vacationed in the mountains near Alta, Utah. While they were on their summer excursion, Nabokov wanted to add to his exquisite and impressive butterfly collection. One day as the famous novelist was pursuing a rare butterfly near a mountain stream at Bear Gulch, he heard the groans of a man in obvious distress. Nabokov ignored the cries for help because he was intent on catching the butterfly to add to his collection. The next day the corpse of a dead prospector was found at the exact location at which Nabokov heard the pleas for help near the stream. Because of this tragic loss of life, the location's name was changed from *Bear Gulch* to *Dead Man's Gulch*. A man lost his life while nearby help was merely chasing butterflies.[3]

Jesus' primary mission was to save lives. "*The Son of Man came not to be ministered unto but to minister and give His life as a ransom for many*" (Mark 12:45). If it was the central focus of my Savior, I need to make it my primary focus. Late one spring afternoon Lisa and I, with our son, chased butterflies in our front yard. It was a wonderful family outing and one that in my mind's eye I still envision. We had a great time chasing the monarchs while Camden followed and laughed the entire time. I still can hear his laughter. But I must never chase butterflies while I ignore the cries of help from neighbors nearby. When you truly love, you share common interests.

### HEARING HIS VOICE

It is shrill and has a distinct sound of its own. I can tell it anywhere—whether we are in a crowded room or in a busy supermarket. I can hear it even in a room filled with other children's voices. In fact I can hear it in the distance right now. It is the sound of my son's voice. I don't have to wait for him to call my name. I can tell his voice immediately. I love hearing it. I love to hear him speak, especially when he has excitement in the tone. The new words he dreams up and tries to vocalize make us laugh. I am amused at hearing him try to repeat words he hears us say.

I didn't set out to memorize his voice. I became very familiar with my son's voice because I heard it so often. I spend so much time with him that I can immediately recognize his voice. The same concept applies with the voice of God. As God's children, the more familiar we become with His voice, the more frequently we will recognize it when we hear it. We will recognize it immediately the more often we hear our Heavenly Father speak to us. We will know His voice when we spend time with Him. We will know it immediately. Jesus said, *"His sheep follow him because they know His voice. But they will never follow a stranger because they do not recognize a stranger's voice"* (John 10:4-5).

Camden didn't speak for quite some time. He walked at 9 months but didn't speak until much later. We began to be concerned about his lack of vocalization. We read articles on the Internet and researched why a child would not be speaking. We tried everything to get him to talk, but for the longest period of time he would not say much. Finally, he began to speak . . . and speak . . . and speak! Now, we have a difficult time imagining we were ever concerned about our son not talking. Hearing his voice is still a wonderful blessing to me.

One of the great blessings of God's people was hearing His voice. In Genesis 3 Adam heard it as he walked with God in the cool of the day. Elijah heard a still, small voice after the wind, fire, and earthquake (1 Kings 19:12). Job declared that God's voice thundered (Job 40:9). Solomon beautifully stated *"the sound of your voice is sweet"* (Song of Solomon 2:14). The Israelites were encouraged to listen when they heard the voice of God (Ps. 95:7). Exiled on the island of Patmos, John received the Revelation and recorded that Jesus said to the church in Laodicea, *"I stand at the door and knock. If anyone hears my voice and opens the door, I will come in and eat with him and he with me*" (Rev. 3:20). Throughout Scripture hearing God's voice was a blessing to His people.

When Camden speaks, I have the responsibility of hearing. When he calls, I am responsible for being there. He cannot do many things for himself. He is too small. He needs me to listen for his voice and respond when I hear it.

The people of God had the responsibility of hearing when God spoke. The Bible repeatedly told the children of God to hear when the Heavenly Father spoke. In one of Israel's great documents known as the *Shema* and found in Deuteronomy 6:4-6, God's people were commanded, "*Hear, O Israel, the Lord thy God is one Lord.*" The very first word of this great document is *hear*. Later Moses commanded the people to listen to God when He spoke (Deut. 18:15). In return God promised to hear when His children spoke (Ps. 34:17).

God spoke to young Samuel while the lad ministered in the Temple. Eli, the priest, encouraged the young boy to return to his bed. But when Samuel heard the voice again, he was to respond by saying, "*Speak, Lord, your servant is listening*" (1 Sam. 3:9). Scripture declares that the earth hears when God speaks (Isa. 65:12). Surely the greatest of all of God's creations—humankind—can hear when the Father speaks. Yet one of the saddest indictments on God's children was from the prophet Isaiah when he stated that God spoke and the people did not hear (Isa. 65:12). In the New Testament, James encouraged believers in Jesus to be swift to hear (Jas. 1:19).

Listening can be a difficult task. In fact we are told that the organ of the body which requires the most energy to operate is the inner ear. One would surmise that perhaps the heart or brain would require the most energy to function properly but, actually, the inner ear requires the most.[4] Listening can be a draining experience which requires focus and attention. Perhaps this fact is why Jesus often repeated the phrase, "*he who has ears to hear, let him hear.*" Yet I have noticed that a person hears much more quickly and readily when attuned to the voice of the one he or she loves. I love my son and listen attentively for his voice. If I love my Lord, I will listen readily and continually for His voice.

I will continue to listen for my son's voice. I want to do so and need to do so. Hearing it is a joy and a blessing. I will continue to recognize it even above all of the other voices I hear. I will hear because it is the voice of my son. I will continue to listen for the voice of God. I want to do so and need to do so. Hearing his voice is a joy and a blessing. I will continue to recognize the voice of God above all of the other voices clamoring for my attention. I will hear it because it is the voice of my Savior. His sheep hear His voice.

## HE IS MINE

Another wonderful surprise of fatherhood was how much I would enjoy simply watching my son sleep. When he is asleep, he is so sweet and adorable! All of my life I heard the joke, "Babies are so sweet . . . when they are asleep", but it really is true. When he is lying there sleeping, you forget about what a terror he was through the day! Such a sweet, serene look on my sleeping son's face is worth the travail of parenting.

Recently as I watched Camden sleep, my mind began to wander. Why do I love this human being so much? Do I love because his actions are always good? Hardly. Do I love him because he is young and helpless? No, other children are young and helpless; I don't have these intense feelings for them. Because he was born to us later in life? Perhaps this fact is somewhat operative here, but I don't believe this is the primary reason.

The reason I love Camden so much is because he is mine. God allowed Lisa and me to bear a child; our union produced something that is ours. Yes, I know that he ultimately belongs to God, but my Heavenly Father has graciously given him to us for a season. He is mine. He is a part of me. He is a part of my heritage. A part of him belongs to my past, certainly to my present, and hopefully to my future. A special relationship is formed just because my son is mine. He is my treasured possession.

I was interested in researching the various Scripture passages in which God told His people that they were His. A special relationship was formed with God and Israel. Above all of the nations of the earth God loved Israel in a special way. The people were His children. Did He love them because their actions were always perfect? Certainly not. Did He love them because they were helpless without Him? Of course not. All nations were helpless without Him. He loved the Israelites simply because He had chosen them to be His children. They were His.

Early on, God established a covenant with His children. On Mount Sinai through Moses God told the people, *"Now, if you obey me fully and keep my covenant, then out of all nations, you will be my treasured possession. Although the whole earth is mine, you will be for me a kingdom of priests and a holy nation"* (Ex. 19:5). What God told the Israelites is very interesting. He said that although all nations were technically His, the Israelites belonged to Him in a special way. Because of this fact they enjoyed a privileged relationship with Him.

In the book of Numbers, God again spoke through Moses and told the Levites they were to be His. Within the Israelites God raised up a subgroup known as the Levites, who were to be the priests. To the Lord they were a special group. *"The Levites are Mine," said the Lord* (Num. 3:12, 45). Later God spoke through His prophets in the Old Testament to remind the Israelites how special they were to Him. In a powerful passage God encouraged a beleaguered Israel after invasions and judgment from opposing nations, *"But now, this is what the Lord says, he who formed you, O Jacob, he who formed you, O Israel. Fear not, for I have redeemed you. I have summoned you by name. You are Mine . . . Since you are precious and honored in My sight and because I love you, I will give men in exchange for you and people in exchange for your life"* (Isa. 43:1, 4).

In later days God used another powerful allegory to reassure an unfaithful Jerusalem that it still was His prized possession. God spoke through the prophet Ezekiel, *"'I spread the corner of My garment over you and covered your nakedness. I gave you My solemn oath and entered into a covenant with you', declares the Sovereign Lord, 'and you became Mine'"* (Ezek. 16:8). Through Malachi during a time of judgment God offered His people hope when He stated, *"They will be Mine, says the Lord Almighty, in the day when I make up my treasured possession"* (Mal. 3:17).

God wanted His people to know they were loved and valued because they were His. They were His treasured possessions. I want my sleeping son to know the same. In our household he is loved, valued, and treasured—for no other reason than because he is mine.

# Chapter 6

# Dependence and Independence

As you travel into Yellowstone National Park, you immediately notice signs advising "Do Not Feed The Bears". Most travelers think the sign is there to warn and protect them from these ferocious animals. Many tourists would think if a bear is close enough to feed, then the bear is close enough to inflict harm on them. Actually the signs are placed in strategic locations throughout the park to protect the bears, not the tourists.

Each fall after the tourists have long since departed, the park service personnel carry off the remains of dead bears they find throughout the park. The bears become so dependent on tourists to feed them, they no longer are able to gather food for themselves.[1]

Right now my son is walking a fine line. The fine line is between dependence and independence. He knows that he is not big enough to do everything for himself and that he must be dependent on us. "Daddddyyyy!" Camden will yell for help throughout our house. "Yes, son," I will respond. "I need your help!" On the other hand he wants to do things for himself. Recently I helped him climb out of our Ford F250 pickup. This can be a difficult climb for a youngster. After I unbuckled him from the car seat, I picked him up and sat him down into our driveway. "No, no, no," Camden said, "I can do it myself!" So my son crawled back up into the pickup and then by himself climbed down out of it. He is exerting his independence and showing me that he now can do some things for himself.

The Christian life is often a fine line between dependence and independence. God desires that I totally depend on Him. But at times He wants me to do things for myself.

## NO BETTER FEELING FOR A FIRST-TIME DAD

I cannot describe what I felt the first time my son placed his arms around my neck and hugged me. It simply was indescribable. Even now as he is older I still feel an unbelievable joy when Camden hugs his daddy. Many times as I get him out of his car seat, he will hug me tightly as we go into the business we're approaching. The feeling is wonderful. I don't know whether fathers who have done this for several years with several children feel the same way. All I know is how a first-time father in his 40s who thought he would never experience the moment feels. I love times when my son depends totally on his father.

When Camden was just a few months old, Lisa and I often lay him between us in bed at his nap time. We turned out the lights and lay beside him while he napped. His tiny fingers reached out into the darkness and found my face. Slowly he ran his tiny fingers over my facial features, as if he were familiarizing himself with them. He began at the top of my head and felt my hair. Then he ran his hand down my face and felt my eyes—first one eye and then the other. Next he felt my nose. For some reason my nose fascinated him the most, so he would spend an extended amount of time there. Then he ran his tiny fingers along my mouth and chin.

After a period of time in which my son felt my facial features, he then fell asleep with his tiny finger wrapped around mine. Even now, as a 3-year-old, Camden will often watch television, listen to a story, or fall asleep with his finger wrapped around my finger. As a first-time father these moments have been pure joy to me. What tremendous joy I have experienced by having my son depend totally on and hold onto me!

As my Heavenly Father, does God experience similar joy? I cannot physically hug my Heavenly Father as my son hugs me, but I wonder whether God basks in those moments when I totally trust Him. He is the One to whom I look for care, sustenance, and support. Of course God wants things that way. I get to know all of the details of my Heavenly Father by spending time with Him and learning of Him, just as my son familiarizes himself with me by physically examining my features.

I am to wrap my finger around God's and hold onto Him, just as my son wraps his finger around mine. Again the image is symbolic. God is a spiritual being rather than a physical one, as John 4:24 tells us. However the Bible consistently uses anthropomorphic language, in which God is given human attributes so we can understand our relationship with Him better.

The finger of God is used as an analogy in Scripture to describe God's formative and creative power.[2] After Moses and Aaron at the command of God placed the plagues on Egypt, the Egyptians declared, *"This is the finger of God"* (Ex. 8:19). Scripture tells us that the Ten Commandments were written with the finger of God (Ex. 31:18). The psalmist said that the beauty and wonder of God's creation is the *work of Your fingers* (Ps. 8:3-4). My son's finger wrapped around mine and my finger wrapped around my Heavenly Father displays total dependence and trust.

## WHY THE ZOO WAS A BENCHMARK FOR ME

I have felt terrible about it ever since it happened. Camden was just over a year old and we were playing at a city park in nearby Allen, TX. It is one of his favorite places to play. Lisa and I were taking him from one play station to another; he was having a good time. He would go from the merry-go-round to the monkey bars to the seesaw. In the far corner of the play area was a small swingset. "Come over here, Boomer, let's swing," I yelled to him. He got into the swing, I stood behind him and began to push him slowly. Suddenly he lost his balance and toppled backward and fell out of the swing before I could catch him. I quickly picked him up, brushed him off, and apologized profusely. The fall didn't hurt him, but it scared him. In fact he didn't even cry, but he was a little hesitant to get back into the swing. I felt badly because I had called him to the swing and then was in position to catch him but didn't do so.

To some degree Camden has always been afraid of heights. So he never really wanted me to carry him on my back or to sit on my shoulders. I felt badly about this, because I remember my father carrying me on his back and what fun that was when I was a child. I wanted my son to have the same joy. Did he not trust me to carry him? I felt hurt to think that may be the case.

Almost one year after the park incident, some close friends asked us to meet them at the Fort Worth Zoo. They have two girls near Camden's age; he always has enjoyed playing with them. We eagerly agreed to meet our friends for a day at the zoo. We had an entertaining day. Camden had a big time seeing the animals and riding the rides. But I will never forget the moment as we were about to leave the zoo when Camden said, "Daddy, will you carry me on your shoulders?" I was overjoyed. "Of course, I will, son. Get on." He climbed onto my back and then on my shoulders. I carried him proudly through the zoo parking lot. We stopped and let him pick leaves from trees and touch signs. The new world of heights was fun to him. He laughed; I beamed as we made our way toward our vehicle to leave the park. "Look, Camden, you are as tall as the giraffe we saw!" He giggled with delight. I carried him all the way back to our vehicle; then we left.

This doesn't sound like much of an event to get excited about, but as a father it was a benchmark for me. The moment meant so much to me because it showed my son's trust in me.

He trusted me to carry him. That trust meant so much to me because I was afraid I had let him down earlier with the swing incident in the park in Allen. He trusted me to carry him on my back. And I was glad to guard that trust.

Now, he wants me to carry him on my shoulders all of the time. One of our weekly rituals is for me to carry my son on my shoulders as we walk through the parking lot as we leave the church after each Sunday's worship service. As we stop, he touches high objects and grabs leaves from the trees. He loves it but not nearly as much as I do! What a joy to carry my son!


## TRUST HIM TO CARRY YOU

The time had been frightening for the Israelites. God's people had fallen. The Assyrian invasion had been difficult on them. Family members had been put to death, property had been destroyed, the land was ravaged, and survivors were taken into captivity. The Assyrian invasion was judgment from the Lord because of the sinfulness of the people. God had warned them, but they failed to repent. So God used an invading army as His instrument to bring His people back to Himself.

The Israelites were wondering whether God could be trusted. Perhaps they felt as Camden did on the Allen playground and wondered whether God truly would catch them when they fell. Yet beginning in Isaiah 40 God spoke to the Israelites words of comfort and reassurance. The days ahead would be a time of restoration and reassurance. Into this context God used the powerful image of a father carrying his child. God could be trusted to carry His people just as a father carried his child. Through the prophet Isaiah God spoke these comforting words, *"Listen to Me, O house of Jacob, all you who remain of the house of Israel, you whom I have upheld since you were conceived, and have carried since your birth. Even to your old age and gray hairs I am He, I am He who will sustain you. I have made you and I will carry you. I will sustain you and I will rescue you"* (Isa. 46:3-4).

In the days ahead the Israelites learned that God indeed was a Father whom they could trust. He carried them faithfully back into their homeland; Jerusalem was restored.

Today's culture can be just as frightening to believers. Christians often wonder how they will manage in the midst of an unstable economy, escalating crime rates, and skyrocketing health-care costs. But the same God who was faithful to carry His people hundreds of years before Christ will carry His children today.

A little boy was once standing on the sidewalk in the middle of a block. For some reason he was obviously waiting there. An older man approached the lad and asked why he was waiting. The boy replied, "I am waiting to catch the bus." The man explained, "Son, the bus doesn't stop here in the middle of the block. If you want to catch the bus, you need to go to the next block and wait at the bus stop." The lad smiled politely and said, "That's OK. I'll wait for the bus right here." The man, wanting to help the lad further, insisted, "Son, you need to go to the bus stop if you want to catch the bus!" A few moments later the bus approached and screeched to halt in front of them. The older man was stunned as the door opened for the child to step on the bus. As the little boy stepped onto the bus, he looked at the older man and said, "I knew the bus would stop to get me. My dad is the bus driver."[3]

The Israelites trusted their Father never to leave or forsake them. They knew He would pick them up and carry them. God's people trusted their Father to remember them. They delighted in the fact that He would carry them where they needed to go. Just as Camden delights for me to carry him, we can trust our Father to carry us.

## HIS HAND IN MINE

My son has always been very independent. Perhaps he is this way naturally. Lisa and I both have always been very independent. Just leave us alone, let us do things for ourselves, and we both are fine. We aren't surprised to discover that the apple didn't fall very far from the tree! Camden is extremely independent.

When he is crossing the street or walking through a parking lot, independence can be a dangerous trait. We constantly instruct him, "Son, hold our hands when you are crossing a street. Always hold our hands whenever cars are nearby." Holding our hands shows a connection to us—a dependence on us in the face of potential danger to him.

He doesn't mind holding our hands. At this age he is content to take hold of our hands and walk alongside us. In fact he often will reach up and grab our hands without our asking him to do so. I noticed that he often does this when he is in a strange environment or in an unfamiliar situation. Holding our hands seems to be a safety net or a security blanket for him. Of course we don't mind. We love to hold our son's hand and feel his tiny fingers holding onto us. We delight in his dependence.

I feel pride when I hold my son's hand as we walk along. Recently I was bringing Camden to our Parent's Day Out program at the church. We got out of our vehicle and began walking, hand-in-hand, toward the facilities. We saw church members in the parking lot and waved to them. I felt such pride as we did so. I am so proud of my son and enjoy walking hand-in-hand with him. We saw some church employees, smiled, and spoke as we entered the church building. They returned the smile and noticed that we were walking hand-in-hand. Again, the moment was a very proud one for me. What a great feeling when my child holds his father's hand and walks with him!

Camden is only 3-years old now. He has not reached the stage in which he feels too old or too independent or too ashamed to hold his parent's hand in public. I know the day will occur. I dread it. I dread the age at which he becomes so independent that he thinks he can do everything for himself. So for now I'll just enjoy the moment. I'll enjoy the time when he walks hand-in-hand and doesn't care what anyone else thinks.

God's hand was powerful in His dealings with His people. The Lord covered Moses with His hand as He hid the servant in the cleft of the rock (Ex. 33:22). Jeremiah felt empowered as God called him to ministry and then reached down and touched the young prophet's mouth with His hand (Jer. 1:9). Later God told His people that much like the clay is in the hand of the potter, they were in His right hand (Jer. 18:6).

God also used his powerful right hand to comfort His people. David was a man who walked hand-in-hand with God and was known as a man after God's own heart. In the psalm he declared, *I stay close to you. Your right hand upholds me* (Ps. 63:8). Another psalmist, Asaph, testified, *Yet, I am always with you. You hold me by my right hand* (Ps. 73:23). Still another psalmist, Ethan, wrote that God said, *My hand will sustain him. Surely My arm will strengthen him* (Ps. 89:21).

Once again God comforted the Israelites after the Assyrian experience. Yet on this occasion the instrument of His comfort was His hand. He told His people, *So, do not fear, for I am with you. Do not be dismayed, for I am your God. I will strengthen you and help you. I will uphold you with my righteous right hand* (Isa. 41:10).

God desires that His children walk hand-in-hand with Him. Sometimes this is for our safety. Our Father knows what potential danger may lie ahead of us just as we know what is best when Camden crosses the street. Walking closely with our child is imperative. So is his holding tightly to our hand. Just as my son doesn't care, right now, who knows he is holding his father's hand, so can I walk with God without fear of who knows of my dependence on Him.

I am sure God delights in our walking hand-in-hand with Him even more than I enjoy my strolls with my son. The pride I feel when I am seen walking hand-in-hand with Camden is likely multiplied many times over when we walk daily with our Father. When we reach up, not because of danger or because we are asked to do so, those times must be the best to Him—times when His children reach up to their Heavenly Father and don't want anything except fellowship. What ultimate joy must radiate in the heart of a loving Father!

### DEPENDENCE AND FAITH

"Where's Mommy?" It's a question I answer at least 25 times a day. Any time that she walks out of his sight, my son wants to know where his mother is. When I am at work, he asks Lisa many times each day, "Where's Daddy?" To my son, reality is only real if you can see it. His mother is only real if he can see her. His daddy exists only if he can see him with his own eyes.

We live on three acres in the country between the cities of Wylie and Sachse. We purchased a home on the acreage because it was one of the few places in the area on which we could enjoy our horses. The deacons of First Baptist Church in Garland built us a horse barn on our acreage. It was a very generous effort; we certainly are grateful. Lisa goes to the barn several times each day to feed the horses or to get items. Every time she goes to the barn, Camden always asks, "Where's Mommy?" He never fails to do so.

One day when my son was only 2-years old and Lisa was feeding the horses, I got the usual query: "Where's Mommy?" I answered with the standard response, "She is at the barn feeding the horses." "But, I can't see her," Camden replied. This time I decided to teach my son a lesson on faith. I called

Camden to my side and said, "Son, just because you cannot see Mommy doesn't mean that she doesn't exist. Look at the barn. Do you see her?" "No," he replied. "But you will see her in just a minute when she returns. She is still very much alive although you cannot see her. She is inside the barn feeding the horses. Son, it is called faith. Faith means you believe in something you cannot see. Just because you cannot see something with your eyes doesn't mean that it isn't real."

I know that he was only 2-years old; I don't know how much of my conceptual analogy he grasped. But early in his life I want to establish the meaning of faith. From his earliest remembrances I want him to hear me say that faith is something we are to possess to please God. I continued my sermon to him, "The Bible tells us that we cannot see God with our eyes. But we know He is real. We believe it by faith. And the Bible tells us that we cannot please God without faith." I'm certain that at 2 he probably didn't understand all of what I was saying. He didn't say anything. He simply looked at me. He had the same look on his face that many of my parishioners have on Sunday mornings! But again I want his earliest remembrances to include his father telling him about faith.

As part of their lesson on dependence God taught His children about faith. To fully please Him He wants them to trust God by faith. They must depend wholly on God to have faith in Him. The writer of Hebrews said, *Now faith is being sure of what we hope for and certain of what we do not see . . . And without faith, it is impossible to please God, because anyone who comes to him must believe that he exists and that he rewards those who earnestly seek him* (Heb. 1:1, 6).

The Lord also taught His children, at an early age, the difference between walking by sight and walking by faith. He placed the Israelites into situations in which they could not see but simply had to follow. He provided manna but only enough for one day. If they tried to gather up manna and store it, then it would ruin. Wouldn't their anxiety been eased if they could have stored up enough for about a month? The apostle Paul stated bluntly to the Corinthians, *We live by faith, not by sight* (2 Cor. 5:7).

During World War II an American plane was flying a mission in Africa. Under the cloak of darkness the aircraft flew toward its destination of Benghazi in North Africa. A fierce tailwind pushed the plane much faster than expected. When the instruments revealed the plane had reached its destination, the flight crew doubted. Their gauges showed their location, but the crew members believed that arriving so quickly was impossible. So the crew chose to ignore its gauges and continued flying. Since the crew members believed the instrument was wrong, they continued on while they looked for a beacon light now miles behind them. Eventually the plane ran out of fuel; the crew perished on impact in the North African desert.[4]

A part of learning to depend on God is to trust Him by faith when our sight and instinct try to convince us otherwise. Trust God—your gauge—even in the dark, since you walk by faith and not sight. It's a lesson God taught His children early and one which unless practiced could have potentially tragic consequences. It is also a lesson I'm attempting to teach my son each time he watches his mommy go out of sight to feed the horses.

### DECLARING HIS INDEPENDENCE

On June 11, 1776, the original 13 Colonies of North America were organized into what was known as the Second Continental Congress. The Congress appointed a group of five men to draft a document justifying reasons to declare their independence. The five men were Thomas Jefferson, John Adams, Benjamin Franklin, Roger Sherman, and Robert Livingston. The group appointed Jefferson to draft the document.

Jefferson spent several agonizing days in Philadelphia trying to word the document precisely. He took the document back to the group of men. In turn on June 28, 1776, the group presented the document to the Continental Congress. The final adoption of the declaration was approved in the early morning hours of July 4, 1776. The document was taken to the Philadelphia printer, John Dunlap. On July 4, 1776, the Declaration of Independence officially was distributed. A nation had declared its independence.[5]

Many times my son has attempted to declare his independence. In fact, now that he is 3, these declarations occur almost daily. Why didn't we simply realize that since he was born on July 4, he was going to be very independent? He certainly is that and very often tries to exert this with us. On many occasions this seems almost to be a calculated power move.

The conversation will go something like this: "Son, don't go outside. It is getting dark and time to come in for the evening." "But, I want to go outside." "No, I said do not go outside." "But, I want to go outside." "Did you hear me?" "But, I want to go outside." "If you walk out of the door, then you will be in trouble." Fortunately, either for us or for him, he doesn't walk out the door. However crying and wailing ensues if he doesn't get what he wants.

I am told that this is common for children his age. They are trying to determine who is in control and how much they control. They are testing boundaries and exerting their independence. In fact many parents tell me that this gets worse when the children become teens! Just great!

In the previous conversation Camden continued to say, "But, I want to . . .." For him the bottom line seems to be that he deserves to get what he wants. He wants us to allow him to do something simply because he wants to do it. And of course as parents we totally disagree. We are staunch and stick by our guns. In fact at times we wonder whether we are too strict. I have heard many parents say they are much more lenient with a second or third child than they are with their first child. I guess Camden is getting our restrictions full-force since he is a first child and we are older.

If we tell him that he cannot do something, then we don't give in and allow him to do it. It is for his good, not necessarily our good. The easiest course of action for us would be simply to let him do what he wants to do. This is the path of least resistance. But it is not for his best. We are convicted that children don't benefit from being reared in an environment in which they get whatever they want, whenever they want it. We truly know what is best for him, although he doesn't understand that fact now. He doesn't understand, so he simply needs to trust us.

At times my son is outright defiant. Thankfully these occasions are rare. They usually occur when he is very tired or does not feel well. But at certain moments when we tell him to do something, he defiantly answers, "NO!" That certainly blesses your heart when children respond that way, doesn't it? "Boomer, it is time for your bath." "NO!" "Don't say 'no' to me! Come here. It is time for your bath." "NO!" To say the least, these times are teachable moments. But his outright defiance calls for our most severe discipline. For him the worst discipline is having privileges taken away. To him the most severe discipline is going to bed early without any juice or snack and not being allowed to watch a cartoon or read a bedtime story. We don't enjoy taking away his privileges. But when he blatantly defies our commands, then we have no choice but to discipline him. Our goal is not to make life easy for him but to make something out of him.

Through my son's obedience, disobedience, dependence, and independence, I have learned so much about my relationship with God. From those moments when I discipline my own son, I have learned about the heart of my Heavenly Father and His discipline. In Chapter 9 I will speak further about discipline.

As believers we often exert our desire to be independent of our Heavenly Father. Often we view His commands as optional. If we don't want to obey them, then much like Camden does, we think not obeying them is acceptable. "But,

I don't want to . . ." we will verbalize or secretly think. God, like a wise parent, knows that always getting our way is not best for His children. He truly knows what is best for us. Understand this fact and trust Him. Simply trusting our Father by faith is in our best interest. That is why the apostle Paul wrote, *All things work together for good to those who love God and are called according to His purpose* (Rom. 8:28).

At other times, much like our son, God's children are blatantly defiant. At times God commands us to obey; we defiantly respond, "NO!" Like a loving parent He often disciplines us most severely when we are blatantly defiant. He often takes our privileges away from us. He doesn't desire to see us hurt. Yet our God knows what truly is best for us. His goal is not to make life easy for us but to make something out of us. His desire is to conform us to the image of His dear Son. And that is always for our best.

# Chapter 7

# A Parent's Pain

My eyes fill with tears each time I watch a television replay of the emotional event—the 1992 Summer Olympics held in Barcelona, Spain. Derek Redmond was one of the favorites to win the gold medal in the 400-meter race. Four years previously Redmond had experienced disappointment when he was forced to withdraw from the same event at the 1988 Summer Olympics held in Seoul, Korea, because of an injury to his Achilles tendon. During the next year Redmond endured five surgeries and painful rehabilitation just to get back to the track.

One of the most powerful figures in Derek's life was his father, Jim. The two were inseparable. They were more than simply a father and son. The Redmonds were extremely close and the best of friends. Each time Derek ran on the track, his father seemed almost to be right beside him and running with him.

As the 400-meter race began in Barcelona, 65,000 screaming fans filling the stadium cheered the runners. More than halfway through the race, Redmond was one of the leaders and was almost assured of placing, which would allow him to advance to the finals. Only 175 meters from the finish line, the Olympian heard a loud pop and felt intense pain in his leg. With his right hamstring snapped, he crumpled to the track. Medical personnel rushed to the fallen athlete and attempted to place him on a stretcher. However, Redmond's father, who had been standing near the top of the stadium, had made his way past security to reach his son lying on the track. The cheering crowd had now fallen silent.

The father ignored medical personnel, made his way to the track, and carefully helped his son to his feet. Jim told Derek, "I'm here, son. We'll finish this race together." Derek Redmond limped painfully slowly toward the finish line with his father's arms wrapped around his waist. For the final 120 meters of the race, people viewed the powerful image of the father and son, arm in arm, limping toward the finish line. Slowly the crowd now began to cheer again. By the time the two crossed the finish line, the crowd was roaring. Now it wasn't about winning a medal. It was about finishing the race. Later in interviews Jim Redmond stated that he had never been more proud of Derek.[1]

Perhaps this sentiment is what the writer of Hebrews was describing as, in this great epistle to Jewish believers, he used the analogy of a race. The Heavenly Father assisted and encouraged His children who were enduring persecution (Heb. 12:1-2). A parent cannot sit back and simply watch a child hurt. Loving parents hurt when their children hurt.

Two recent experiences saddened me. The first was an interview I heard on a news program on television. On a news talk show the parents of a 21-year-old young woman were interviewed. She had been missing for 10 days and was presumed to have eloped with her boyfriend. The boyfriend had been on a killing spree; the young woman simply went along for the journey. The couple is still wanted nationwide and among America's Most Wanted fugitives. Throughout the interview I was captivated by the hurt evident in the missing girl's parents. Their eyes looked hollow, obviously from a lack of sleep. Their voices barely were above a whisper. Their body language communicated defeat. Their physical features displayed the obvious hurt only parents could feel.

The second experience was a conversation I had with a woman who had just discovered that her son had cancer. Between her sobs I counseled with the woman. Actually in my vocation I have many such conversations, but this particular conversation struck a chord with me. I always have hurt for the parents, but I hurt much more deeply now that I am a father. I was especially struck by the pain of the mother. I could sense in her voice a great deal of fear, questions, anxiety, and most of all, hurt. Although I have never experienced a child's rebellion and leaving home nor a devastating illness to happen to my child, I still believe that no greater pain than that of a parent must exist.

## AN EYE-OPENER AT MCDONALD'S

I'll never forget an incident that happened one Sunday morning after church. Camden had just turned 2-years old. The day seemed to be a normal Sunday. Often we stop by McDonald's for Sunday lunch on the way home from church. No, it is not my choice for a fancy Sunday meal, but it is easy with a 2-year-old. Camden can play in the play area, while Lisa and I relax and visit. We can eat our Happy Meals in peace while he burns some energy. Then, we can all go home and enjoy Sunday-afternoon naps. It works pretty well for us.

On this particular Sunday, we took the short drive to the McDonald's on North Garland Avenue just down the street from our church. I ordered the food while Lisa went into the play area with Camden. He seemed to be quieter than usual but didn't appear in a bad mood. Lisa and I sat down at a table to enjoy our hamburger and French fries. About three bites into the meal, I noticed that Lisa jumped from the table, dashed into the play area, and was telling Camden "no." I looked in time to see my son pounding on another little boy. Lisa pulled him off of the little boy and asked Camden what the problem was, but he didn't respond. We told him to play nice and not to be hitting. I was wondering where he had witnessed such violence. He certainly doesn't see physical abuse in our home and doesn't watch violent television programs.

Lisa sat back down at the table to continue our meal and simply shook her head. About five bites of hamburger later, I turned to check on my boy and noticed that he was at it again! There he was, pounding on the same little boy. This time, Lisa and I both rushed to the rescue to give the other boy some relief.

About the same time the boy's mother arrived at the scene. We separated the boys and again scolded Camden for not obeying us and for hitting the little boy. Again our son offered no explanation and was unusually silent. This time, the mother took her child, glared at us, and left the restaurant. We felt badly and were perplexed as to why he was acting this way.

Lisa and I returned to our table and began to discuss what was going on with him. About five more bites into our meal, we noticed that Camden was now beating on another little boy. I couldn't believe what I was seeing! Once again my wife and I both rushed to the rescue and separated the boys. We had had enough. We forgot about lunch, took Camden outside, scolded him again, and went home. We continually asked him why he was acting in this manner, but he refused to answer and remained unusually quiet.

Fortunately he has not been in one of these moods since this day, but I will never forget my feeling. For the first time I felt the pain of a parent whose child was hurting someone else. Until now we had heard nothing but positive comments about our son. We heard doting comments about our "wonderful" son, which often happens when a person is in a higher-profile church position.

I often wonder what the real truth is about my son. I guess as a parent you want to believe all of the nice words and not think that your son is capable of hurting anyone else. But on this day I left McDonald's with an odd feeling. This child of mine, for whom I felt so much love, had deliberately hurt other children. My heart hurt deeply over the fact that he had done so.

## THE PAIN OF CAUSING PAIN

Little Jeffrey Lionel was born only one month after I was. He was born into this world at 4:34 p.m. on May 21, 1960, at Evangelical Deaconess Hospital in Milwaukee, WI. His parents were proud and doted on their new baby. Lionel and Joyce adored and loved their little boy just as many other couples have done for years. Lionel worked in a downtown Milwaukee laboratory; Joyce worked as a teletype operator, but they made time to shower their new baby with love and attention. As Jeffrey grew, Joyce kept a scrapbook of his "firsts". She recorded his first step, kept his first tooth, detailed his first accident, and kept locks from his first haircut. Little did Lionel and Joyce Dahmer know that their son, Jeffrey, would grow up to become one of America's most infamous serial killers and necrophiliacs. Between 1978 and 1991 Jeffrey Dahmer killed and dismembered 17 men and boys before he cannibalized them.[2]

I watched a television documentary in which Dahmer's parents were interviewed at length after his conviction, imprisonment, and ultimate murder in a Wisconsin penitentiary. They spoke in detail about Jeffrey's childhood, teen years, and young adult life. As they spoke, the deep hurt and intense pain was evident. They were hurt and embarrassed because their last name had become synonymous with that of a monster.

During the interview with the Dahmers I observed something interesting. During most of the dialogue when the topic of the victims surfaced, Lionel and Joyce Dahmer wept the most. They both agreed that they hurt over what their son became. However they both also agreed that the greatest hurt they felt through the entire experience was the pain and suffering their son had caused. What hurt their hearts deeply was the pain inflicted on other parents' sons and on other parents through the actions of Jeffrey. During this portion of the documentary they wept intensely. They obviously felt the pain about the fact that someone they loved had caused pain.

Obviously I have never felt the type of parental pain that Lionel and Joyce experienced. I pray that I never will. Occasionally I have seen Camden hit another child as they are playing with the same toy. Of course we always chastise him for such actions, but our hearts hurt when we see him trying to hurt others.

I have always enjoyed the beautiful prayer (1 Chron. 4:10) offered by a man named Jabez. He lived during an uneventful time in Judah's history. This godly man offered a simple, straightforward prayer which God blessed. Scripture tells us that Jabez was more honorable than were his brothers. He cried out to God. *"Oh, that you would bless me and enlarge my territory! Let your hand be with me, and keep me from harm so that I will be free from pain."* God granted his heartfelt request. I love this prayer because of its simplistic approach yet heartfelt passion. I'm not a fan of the commercialization associated with it in the last few years. I'm uncertain whether God designed this prayer to be a formula to follow for 30 days and your life will be blessed. Jesus warned us against vain repetitions and trying to turn our relationship with Him into ritual. This wonderful prayer has been turned into a magical incantation by many who try to invoke God's blessings on their lives. I just like reading the simple, heartfelt prayer of a man desiring to please God.

The part of I love the most is the powerful ending of the prayer. The New International Version interprets the final phrase of the prayer *"so that I may be free from pain."* However the most literal Hebrew rendering of the phrase literally implies *"that I may not cause pain."* Jabez asked God to keep him from being the source of pain to others.

The final phrase in the prayer of Jabez has also been my prayer for quite some time. I do not want to be the cause of pain to another person. I want to be a blessing rather than a pain. My desire is the same for my son. I hurt deeply when he wants to hurt others. "Father, may my son, my wife, and I each be used as instruments of blessing rather than pain."

# WHEN OTHERS HURT MY SON

On June 28, 2006, a cool evening in Bountiful, UT, the lights were bright under the Utah stars as the large crowd assembled for the championship game of the Mueller Park Mustang Baseball League. This league featured baseball players 10-years of age and under. The championship game promised to be a good one. The undefeated Yankees were playing the Red Sox in a grudge match to see which team reigned supreme and had bragging rights for one more year.

As advertised the game was close. In the bottom of the last inning the Yankees held a one-run lead. The Red Sox were at bat with the tying run on third base and two outs. The feared hitting star, Jordan Bleak, was approaching the plate for the Red Sox. Bleak already had hit a three-run home run and a triple in the game. Red Sox parents were expecting him to at least tie and possibly win the game. All of a sudden Yankee managers did something unprecedented which caused the entire nation to buzz.

Yankee managers went to the pitcher's mound to have a conference with their star pitcher. They discussed the on-deck hitter who would bat after Bleak. It was 9-year-old Romney Oaks. Oaks had recently survived surgery and chemotherapy after a vigorous bout with brain cancer. His condition left him weakened. While he played in the outfield, he had to wear a protective helmet to guard a shunt implanted in his head.

In an unprecedented move Yankee managers ordered their pitcher to walk intentionally Bleak so the weakened Oaks would have to bat with the game on the line. The managers were well within the rule book to walk a batter intentionally, but the coaches had an unwritten rule that, at this age level, they would not do so. Despite the unwritten rule Bleak was intentionally walked and Romney Oaks batted with the championship on the line.

Being in a weakened condition, Oaks was no match for the power pitcher of the Yankees. The young cancer survivor swung at the first pitch but was nowhere close to making contact. Tears began to fill his eyes. Oaks swung woefully and missed the second fastball right over the plate. Tears now began to trickle down the little boy's cheeks as the thought of striking out with the championship on the line raced through his mind. Later he said that he was crying because he did not want to disappoint his teammates. The Yankee pitcher fired another fastball but, once again, the young boy's swing was nowhere near the ball. Oaks had struck out with the tying run on third base and winning run on first base. The Yankees celebrated wildly on the field. Oaks no longer was able to hold back his emotions as he sobbed uncontrollably on the field.

Sports magazines and national talk shows discussed the lack of professionalism of the Yankee coaches in wanting to win at all costs. Why would adults intentionally place a 9-year-old survivor of brain cancer in a situation where they could take advantage of his weakened condition just to win a baseball game?[3]

As I heard this story, I found myself angry. I listened intently to the talk-show debates and wondered how I would feel if Romney Oaks were my son. What if Camden were the one that opposing managers took advantage of after he had just finished cancer treatment? I was angered even more when I envisioned the scenario happening to Camden. Few things rouse the ire of parents more than does someone trying to harm their child.


### ANOTHER MCDONALD'S EXPERIENCE

Once again we were all at a fast-food restaurant for Sunday lunch. And, yes, it was a restaurant with a play area for children while the parents can sit down, relax, and enjoy a meal while the children play. For the first 18 years of our marriage Lisa and I never even knew such restaurants existed. We never noticed whether an eating establishment had a play area.

Quite frankly, had we known such places existed, we probably would have wondered why. Now we look for them! We were pretty settled into a routine of marriage and family life, but now a little boy has totally changed how we view everything, including dining out.

Once again we sat at a table in the play area and were relaxing after a Sunday-worship service. Suddenly we noticed a commotion surrounding Camden. We saw activity and heard harsh words. Lisa jumped up from the table first; I was close behind as we headed to the play area. We suspected that perhaps our son was beating on another child again. But when we arrived this time, something entirely different was taking place. The tables were completed turned. This time Camden was the recipient of another child's aggression. I saw another boy pounding our son. One blow after another was landing; Camden was trying to fend for himself but not doing too well.

The emotions that I felt totally surprised me. I felt completely different than before when son was beating another child. I felt hurt, disappointment, responsibility, and compassion when Camden was the aggressor. Yet now my feelings had gone 180 degrees. I felt anger, vengeance, and hostility. I wanted to fight back personally and stop the little boy from hurting my son. I was bigger and stronger than the young child. I could have restrained him and stopped the entire incident personally. What was the little boy doing? Didn't he know that this was our precious son? Wasn't he aware that we were childless for years, didn't think we could have children, and were given an absolute miracle? Didn't he realize this boy is special? Of course he did not, nor should he. These simply were quick, fleeting thoughts as I separated the two boys.

Later in the day as I reflected on the incident, God spoke to my spirit. He impressed on me to reflect on the cross. Scripture never tells us how God the Father responded when His Son Jesus was being beaten and crucified. Some theologians have wondered if the strange acts of nature, i.e. the sun being darkened, the earthquake, etc., were God's way of speaking and voicing displeasure at the events. Quite possibly they were. Yet we are never told overtly about God's response during the trial, beatings, and crucifixion of Jesus.

How did God feel when His only begotten, precious Son was being attacked? What was His response to the beard of Jesus being plucked, the fists pounding on Him, the spittle running down His cheeks, the crown of thorns on His brow, the lashes upon His back, and the nails in the hands and feet? Did He have the same urge to jump in and stop the attack? He could have done so. In the snap of a finger He could have sent angels and stopped the events. But He didn't. This fact spoke volumes to me. Although other people were hurting His Son, He didn't stop the events from unfolding. Why didn't He stop the attack? Love. Love for me. Love for my wife. Love for my little boy. Love for you. Love even for the ones participating in the attack. Perhaps more love was necessary for Him to refrain than for Him to act.

Did God have the same thoughts as I did when He witnessed the attack? Did He want to say, "What are you doing? Don't you realize that this is My only, precious Son? Aren't you aware that His birth was a miracle as God incarnate and that He is a special man? Don't you realize how special He is as the King of glory?" Of course they did not realize it. Oh, they did so after the fact, when a Roman centurion looked at the cross and confessed, *"Truly this was the Son of God"* (Mt. 27:54 KJV), but they didn't realize this crucifixion's magnitude.

At times in Scripture, God's people called out and He responded quickly. The Israelites were in bondage and needed relief from Pharaoh's hand. They later needed His assistance to defeat the Philistines—again and again. Gideon needed God to help him quickly defeat the Midianites. The list goes on and on. Many times in Scripture, God's children needed their Father to aid them and to stop an attack from an aggressor. He quickly and willingly did so. Yet at the cross He did not. What restraint from a Father!—all the more reason my God has my admiration and deep love.

## WHAT DOES THIS PHRASE MEAN?

The governor's soldiers took Jesus into the Praetorium as the crowd gathered around Him (Mt. 27:37). They stripped Him of His clothes, put a scarlet robe on Him, and twisted together a crown of thorns for His head. Next they placed a scepter in His right hand and knelt in mock homage to Him. They spat on Him, struck Him with their fists again and again, and led Him away to be crucified (Mt. 27:28-31).

The soldiers forced Jesus to carry His cross to Golgotha for the crucifixion. Weakened from the beating he fell beneath the load. Simon of Cyrene carried the cross for Him (Mt. 27:32). Once at Calvary, the soldiers drove spikes into His right and left hands. One longer spike was driven through both feet, with one foot placed on top of the other and fastened to the cross.

Jesus was placed on the cross at the sixth hour, according to how the Jews calculated time. In our culture this would correspond to 9 a.m. He hung on the cross for six hours. While He hung on the cross, Jesus spoke seven words or phrases. Since I am a father, my attention is captured by the sixth of these seven phrases.

About the ninth hour, or noon, Jesus cried out with a loud voice, *"Eloi, Eloi, lama sabachthani?"* The phrase was in the Aramaic language, which was one of at least two languages Jesus spoke. The phrase meant, *"My God, My God, why have you forsaken Me?"*

I realize that Jesus was quoting Psalm 22:1. But a greater significance to the statement has to exist than simply quoting Scripture. Jesus did nothing without purpose. Did God the Father truly abandon Jesus in the hour in which His Son needed Him the most?

Our nation has a serious and growing problem with absentee fathers. We have 24.7 million children who live without their biological fathers in their homes, which is 32 percent of the entire United States population. In fact in a recent survey of Americans, 72 percent of our population believes that the situation with absentee fathers is the number-one problem facing families today.⁴ Often when the children need their fathers the most, these dads are absent. Was God an absentee Father at the cross?

God the Father is holy. Jesus is eternal and knew only perfect fellowship with His Heavenly Father. The incarnate Jesus became subordinate to the Father, humbled Himself, and became obedient, even to the point of obedience to the cross (Phil. 2:8). Jesus became sin for us as our atoning sacrifice. He actually became our sin. From the most innocent of sins, in our eyes, to the most heinous, Jesus became our sin. Jesus literally became our sin on the cross. Otherwise no atonement would be available to us. God loves, but He is also just. Payment had to be made.

A holy God could not look on the sin which Jesus had become as He hung on the cross. It was as if God the Father turned His back or turned away from the sin. Having never known separation from the Father for even one moment, Jesus hardly could bear the distance. He could hardly bear the thought of separation from the Father as He anguished over the broken fellowship which sin had caused.

We are not told the Father's feelings during this experience. We are told how Jesus the Son felt, but not how God the Father felt. I wonder whether leaving His Son on the cross and turning away was difficult. In the heart of a loving, perfect Father, what did that feel like?

Quite often Camden calls out for me. "Daddddyyyy," I hear very frequently. If I hear him and am physically able, I respond. In fact I now had to stop writing this text because he was calling for me to open the security gate so he could walk upstairs to be with me while I wrote. "Daddy, I need you!" That phrase is all I need to hear; I will drop what I am doing to help. I love for him to depend on me. I am delighted that I can be of assistance to him. Helping him is a wonderful feeling. A true joy of fatherhood is hearing the shrill, squeaky voice of my son asking his father for help. I can't help wondering what the experience of the cross was like for God the Father. God has taught me so much about Himself and how the ultimate Father feels, thinks, and acts. The cross must have been just as difficult for the Father as it was for the Son. I am so thankful God loves me as much as He does.


## WHEN MY SON HURTS ME

This is difficult for me to admit. I have never told anyone about an incident when my son was 2-years old and my subsequent feelings about it. I guess I might as well bare it before you now.

Camden had just awakened from a late-afternoon nap. We try to discourage these late-afternoon naps so he will go to bed earlier, but sometimes we cannot avoid them. On this particular day he awakened in a bad mood. Nothing pleased him; no one satisfied him with anything. Lisa needed to run to the grocery store, so Camden was going to stay with me. He wanted to go with her rather than staying home with Dad. She told him that he could not go; he threw a fit. I mean, he proceeded to throw an authentic, 2-year-old temper tantrum. He didn't get his way and, right there in the driveway of our home, he wanted everyone to know how he felt.

"I want to go with Mommy to the store! I don't want to stay home with Daddy!" He kept shouting this over and over. Lisa chided him and then scolded him and told him that he was not going to get his way. She simply got into the vehicle and drove away to the store. As she was getting into the vehicle and all the time she was pulling out of the driveway, my son kept shouting, "I don't want you, Daddy! I don't want you, Daddy!"

Camden was not a happy camper as we walked back into the house and Lisa drove away. I tried to interest him in playing with some of his toys, but he was in no mood. We tried reading stories, which he rarely rejects. He sat there with a scowl. He was not happy and wanted to let me know of his extreme displeasure. I was just as determined as him not to let him win this battle.

I admit that he had hurt me. I didn't let him know, but my feelings were hurt deeply. I still can recall the event and all of the details vividly in my mind's eye now. I still can hear the phrase ringing across our lawn: "I don't want you, Daddy!" Even months later my heart hurts again, as I reflect on the event and on that ringing phrase.

Now, I know all of the reasons why he made these statements. He had just awakened and was in a bad mood. He was 2-years old and simply trying to figure out the boundaries of his independence. He wanted to know whether he would get his way. He did not get his way and was lashing out. The only way he knew to hurt back was by stating his displeasure. He didn't mean the statement about not wanting me. We have a wonderful relationship; we love each other. In my head I know all of these facts. But the facts didn't stop my heart from hurting because of his statements.

I serve as the senior pastor of a congregation of more than 5,200 members. Almost every day I make decisions which have the potential to be criticized. I will never please all of the members of the congregation; I am well aware of this fact. Criticism is part of the territory and hardly fazes me. Through the empowering of the Holy Spirit and after gathering all of the facts, I make the best decisions possible and live with them. And I had my feelings hurt by a 2-year old? I felt rather foolish, actually. The temper tantrum of a 2-year-old had hurt my feelings. But the feeling was different with Camden. It was my son telling me that he didn't want me. The words hurt deeply.

Later, as God always seems to do, He spoke gently to my spirit. What about the times I have not wanted to be with my Heavenly Father? What about the times in which I have not wanted to have a daily devotional time or spend time in Bible study and prayer? I have never shouted, "I don't want you, God!" But my actions have shown that I have not wanted Him. Does my lack of desire for Him hurt the heart of my loving Heavenly Father? I had never envisioned this before. I bowed my head and prayed, "Dear Lord, I don't want to hurt your heart. I want to learn a lesson from how I felt about my son's tantrum. May I never become angry with You because I did not get my way and try to lash back at You. I never want to hurt your heart, Father."

## THE WOUNDED PARENT

In more than 27 years of pastoral ministry I have counseled with many parents about their children. The phrases have been oft-repeated through the years. "My child is literally breaking my heart." "If they only realized how deeply this is hurting me." "I don't think I can bear the actions of my child any longer." "What my child is doing now is the most difficult thing I've ever been through in my life."

Parents often experience private pain when their children are concerned. Something about the pain a child causes a parent is unlike any other pain the parent has felt. I did not realize the depth of such parental pain before I had a child but certainly can envision it much more acutely now.

Parental pain often was mentioned during my interviews with ministers in research for this book. The most frequent response of the ministers, when I asked them the greatest challenges of parenthood, centered on watching their children struggle. Allowing a child to fail was very difficult for the ministers to go through. One minister said, "It was tough to watch my child's failure and resulting hurt. It was even tougher to sit back and not jump in to help when you wanted to get involved. It made me view the cross differently."

Dr. Guy Greenfield taught my Christian Ethics class during my master's level studies at Southwestern Baptist

Theological Seminary in Fort Worth. I enjoyed his class and learned from him. Early in his life Dr. Greenfield experienced personal pain. As a youth he faced one obstacle after another. Yet he stated that the pain a parent feels about his or her child is the worst pain of all.

In his book, *The Wounded Parent*, Dr. Greenfield discussed how parents can cope with children who have disappointed them.[5] Often, children will reject the values, morals, and belief system in which they were reared. Other children will engage in moral or ethical behavior which is contrary to the value system in which they were reared. In many situations children will disappoint parents. These wayward children literally break the hearts of parents. Dr. Greenfield has been such a parent and counseled many others in similar situations.

As I mentioned, I have been hurt at times by certain actions and attitudes of my son. He is only 3-years old now. I haven't even scratched the surface of the hurt experienced by a parent who has had a child die. I have never gone through the grief a wayward teen can bring to a home. Over time I possibly could experience one or both situations. I am not immune from either simply because I am a minister. Such pain must be devastating.

My sister and brother both have adult children. They are sitting back and enjoying "little brother" with his first small child. At times I think they have way too much enjoyment watching my struggles! But they keep telling me that my experiences now are the easy years. "Just wait until Boomer is a teen-ager," they keep telling me. Perhaps I'll need to write a sequel to this book when my son hits the teen years! I'm certain that during those years I will learn even more about God!

As I reflect on parental pain, I think of my Heavenly Father. I am certain that my actions and attitudes often hurt the heart of God, although Scripture doesn't give me much insight into all my Heavenly Father is feeling when I sin. Admittedly I never thought much about parental pain before I was a father. I am acutely aware of it now. During our preg-

nancy the thought of how my son may possibly hurt me someday never even entered my mind. I never even considered it
once. But my brief experience as a father has made me keenly
aware of how I hurt my Father. It has changed me. I never
want to cause my Heavenly Father pain.

# Chapter 8

# Teaching Him to Walk

David Kunst of Waseca, MN, was the first person to do it. With his brother beside him David set out on June 20, 1970, with the goal of walking around the entire world. For the next four-and-a-half years he put one foot in front of the other to accomplish this lofty goal. He faced constant dangers and endless fatigue. On one occasion bandits in Afghanistan shot Kunst. His brother was killed in the attack; David survived only by playing dead. On October 5, 1974, Kunst finally reached his goal of circumventing the globe. He was the first person officially certified as having walked completely around the world. In the process Kunst wore out 22 pairs of shoes while he was on the 14,450-mile journey. Quite simply his lengthy endeavor began with the very first step.[1] Most of us will never walk completely around the world. But as we grow, learning to walk is a vitally important event. What a special time Camden's learning to walk was!

## A SPECIAL TIME

I had always envisioned what teaching a child to walk was like. For 18 years I thought I would never be able to experience this wonderful joy of parenthood. Secretly I was bothered that I would never get to enjoy some of these special times as a father, but I accepted the plight as God's plan for us. My faith was strong enough that I knew with certainty that if God desired I become a father, then He would allow this to take place. If God did not desire that for me, then I accepted it as well.

What would teaching your child to walk be like? I wondered. How would I feel when my child takes those first steps? I could only try to imagine. From time to time through the years I wondered such questions and prayed that some day I would be able to experience these joys as a father. Then I would dismiss the thought so as to not get my hopes up in case it never happened. I accepted the fate and trusted that God knew best.

On the day when Lisa and I found out for certain that we were pregnant, my mind began to envision all of the blessings which I may now get to experience. *I may get to enjoy all of these blessings that I thought for years I would never be able to experience*, I thought. On the day we found out that Lisa was pregnant, one of the great blessings I anticipated was being able to teach my child to walk one day. I don't know why it meant so much to me. But I wanted to enjoy this process.

I don't know why Camden's walking was so much more important to me than was his talking or other aspects of child development. Perhaps this is because the Bible places so much emphasis on walking. In Scripture the analogy of walking is used to describe many important events. Walking was analogous to fellowship with God. God walked with Adam in the cool of the day. Enoch walked with God. God walked with His people. Scripture tells us that God taught His children to walk. The Bible warns us about walking in the paths of the unrighteous and implores us to walk in the right ways. Now I apparently would be able to enjoy the blessings of a father teaching his child to walk. God has certainly been good to me.

Of course a child all of a sudden one day doesn't just begin walking. A series of other events precede this monumental milestone. Each of these events helps strengthen muscles and develop control in an infant. First a child reaches for and grasps objects when they are held out to him or her. The average age at which a baby accomplishes this task is about 4-months old. At an early age Camden seemed to master this feat. Also at about 4 months of age, infants learn to hold their heads erect. Next, when their trunk is supported, they begin to sit up at about 8 months of age. Again Camden accomplished these feats earlier than did the average child. In general the average age for a child to begin walking is 15 months.[2] I deducted that since our son accomplished these activities early, then quite possibly he would also begin walking early.

Lisa and I are deeply indebted to a family who since his birth has helped us with Camden. Larry and Carol Thompson have been like grandparents to him. They live in Iowa Park and were members of Faith Baptist Church when I served as pastor there. The Thompsons have kept Camden frequently for us. He has become like a member of their family. Having such great friends nearby who could keep our son was wonderful, since both sets of our parents are deceased and the remainder of our family lived several hours away. The Thompsons have served in this role well. We are thankful for them.

I wasn't present when Camden took his first step. He was at the Thompsons' home. When he took his first step, they were babysitting for us. He didn't crawl for very long before he began to walk. At nine months of age my son took his first step. But being present at the first step wasn't as important to me as was being involved in the process of teaching him how to walk throughout the course of time.

Teaching him to walk was a wonderful experience! First we would stand him on his feet and hold up his hands. He wanted to walk and tried to push forward but couldn't seem to do so. Next we would balance his momentum as he held his hands above his head; we would hold on. Many, many times I had seen other parents hold their children in this manner. Now I was getting to hold my child like this.

Before long Camden was very slowly placing one foot in front of the other. I would walk along with him while he held his hands above his head; he would walk slowly. I didn't mind that he couldn't go very fast. I experienced great joy holding onto his hands while he took those all-important steps. I'd wait patiently for the next step to land. The process was slow and tedious, but each step was joyful for me.

Later Camden grew more confident with his steps. I would continue to hold his hands above his head and walk with him, but he was walking a little more confidently and faster. Next he was walking very well on his own but still wanted me above him holding his hands and taking the steps along with him. For many years I had envisioned this moment. It was everything I had imagined and even more.

Finally one day he turned loose of my hands and began walking on his own. The moment was bittersweet. I was delighted to watch my child walk. But I experienced a tinge of sadness as well. I know that the ultimate goal was for him to become independent and do things for himself. He needed to be walking on his own. Yet I enjoyed his dependence on me that he needed to get where he was going. I actually loved to hold up his hands and walk with him.

Now, at 3-years old, Camden runs. He runs almost every-where he goes. He squeals with delight as he runs outside and when Patches, our dog, runs with him. What a joy to see Camden enjoy himself! When he is inside the house, I hear the pitter-patter of his little feet that move as quickly as possi-ble while they pound our floor in excitement. He is excited to show us something. We can hear him approaching us; what a wonderful sound! I know that we will not always hear that sound. As he continues to grow, that beautiful sound of little feet running will not be heard. When that magical sound fades, the time will be sad for us. I dread the time already. I'm sure that in our home, the silence will be deafening. But as for now, we still hear that wonderful sound and love it.

Life has really been a true adventure for Lisa and me. Eighteen years without children. Both of her parents had died. My mother had died; my father was about to die. God blessed us with a child who was healthy and full of life. And the pitter-patter of our son's feet was filling our home. We both wished that our parents could enjoy his walking and running as much as we did. For us the time was both joyous and sad.

In 2004 singer Alan Jackson recorded a song entitled "Remember When." A few of the lines really fit our lives:

> "Remember when . . . old ones died and new were born,
> And life was changed, disassembled, rearranged?
> Remember when . . . the sound of little feet was the music,
> We danced to week to week?
> We won't be sad, we'll be glad, for all the life we've had,
> And we'll remember when."[3]

## A POWERFUL ANALOGY

One of my favorite Old Testament books is Hosea. It became one of my favorite biblical books during my course of study at Oklahoma Baptist University. Under the brilliant teaching of the late Dr. Dick Rader I learned so much about this eighth-century prophet. As part of my degree plan for a bachelor's degree in religion I took a course entitled "Amos and Hosea." I enjoyed the class so much that when I was working on my master of divinity degree at Southwestern Baptist Theological Seminary, I took another class with the same title. Dr. Dan Kent was able to delve deeper into these two powerful books. After these two courses I considered Hosea to be one of the most powerful books of Scripture because of the vivid imagery God uses to describe His love for His children.

Hosea lived during the final, tragic days of the northern kingdom. As judgment for the sins of her people Israel was invaded by the awesome Assyrian armies. God had warned the Israelites that judgment was approaching if they did not repent of their evil actions and return to Him. They refused to repent, so the dark clouds of judgment loomed on the horizon.

The Assyrians attacked the Israelites in waves. In 733 B.C. this Semitic nation was essentially dismembered.[4] Wounded and bleeding God's people limped along but still refused to repent. The Assyrians captured the northern kingdom with a deliberate and fatal attack on Samaria. The remaining residents of the country were exiled. In 722 B.C. the northern kingdom officially ended.

Into this historical setting God called the prophet Hosea. He called him not only to preach His message but to mirror the Father's steadfast love for His children. In spite of their failures the Israelites were still God's children. God was not giving up on them. Hosea's personal life was to be an illustration of God's relationship with Israel.

Hosea was to marry a prostitute named Gomer. When this husband and wife had children, they were to name their offspring surprising names. It was God's way of telling His covenant people, "I am married to an unfaithful people and I am disappointed in you." Throughout the fateful book God told the Israelites the details of the consequences of their sin.

Yet God's unfailing love for His people made His giving up on them impossible. Gomer became unfaithful to Hosea, but he was to pursue her and to bring her back home. She went back to her ways of prostitution and was sold into the slave market. But Hosea loved her faithfully and bought her back from slavery. In spite of all Hosea had done, she continued to be unfaithful. The Israelites must have gotten the picture. Through Hosea's marriage and family life the analogy of God's relationship with His people was mirrored strikingly.

In Chapter 11 of this great book God seemed to become rather nostalgic. He began to reminisce about the wonderful days in which Israel was only an infant and depended totally on Him. The Father thought back on the early days of His relationship with Israel. He went all the way back to a stage in Israel's history in which His children were about Camden's age. They were infants and totally dependent. God longed for the days in which Israel was an infant again. With powerful imagery God spoke in longing terms for the "good old days."

*When Israel was a child, I loved him . . .* (Hos. 11:1). I am certain that Lisa and I will look back longingly on the days in which Camden was an infant. We will always love him, as God always loved His children, but the powerful love of a parent is exceptionally strong when children depend on you.

*It was I who taught Ephraim to walk, taking them by the arms* (Hos. 11:3). As I related in Chapter 1, *Boomer* is our affectionate, pet name for Camden. *Ephraim* was God's personal, pet name for Israel. God was remembering the close, intimate fellowship He experienced with Israel before its fall. God used the analogy of teaching a child to walk to describe His close connection with them. My experience of holding Camden's arms while he was learning to walk was the image God used to describe His former relationship with Israel. It was as special a time for God as it was for me.

God continued with beautiful, poetic words, *I led them with cords of human kindness, with ties of love. I lifted the yoke from their neck and bent down to feed them.* God used the concept of a father's tender love for an infant to describe how He felt about Israel, His children. I indeed have been blessed by being allowed to experience this same special bond.

## A DEMANDING FATHER?

Recently I officiated at the funeral service of one of the members of our church. At the cemetery in the shade of the hot, Texas sun, after the service I visited at length with a family member of the deceased. Mostly we talked about Christianity and church life. The woman, in her mid-60s, described to me the church in which she was reared. The pastor was large, his voice boomed, and he often preached on the judgment of God. She told me that for many years she feared her Heavenly Father because of this image of God her pastor portrayed to her. She spoke of the liberty she experienced a few years ago when she finally learned of her Heavenly Father's loving side.

This morning I stopped typing this manuscript because of an appointment I had with a woman who has been visiting our church. As we sat and talked, she described her past to me. The woman went into great detail in describing her father. She never felt loved by him. He was stern, harsh, and demanding. The woman admitted that she feared him. She confessed, "I was afraid of my father all the time I was growing up. He scared me to death. In fact even as an adult I feared him." She was especially afraid to admit to him any mistake she may have made or to confess any fault. He was unforgiving and very demanding. This image of her father carried over into her concept of God. She also viewed God as harsh and demanding. She told me that she never has truly believed that God has forgiven her for any of her past sins.

Is God's character as these women perceived for many years? Is He harsh, demanding, difficult to please, and eager to strike down the first person who steps out of line? Is God a mean, unforgiving father you are afraid even to approach, much less to confess a sin?

The fact that God's people often portray our Heavenly Father in such a light is unfortunate. Yes, He is a God of justice. Yes, He upholds a standard which He does not relax. Yes, He is a God who demands accountability from His children. But God also extends mercy in the face of judgment. He offers grace in the midst of justice. How is God defined? Words such as *just, condemning,* or *judgmental* were not used when Scripture defined God's very nature. Instead the word *love* was used (1 John 4:8). Many people miss out on the loving and forgiving God whom Jesus portrayed.

If I want to know how God feels as a Father, I can examine my own feelings as a father. Please don't misunderstand me. I am not saying that I am the same kind of father as God is. I am not nor will I ever be the perfect father. He is perfect; I am sinful. As a father I do wrong things, become angry, and develop wrong attitudes. But He is the One who used the analogy of a father to describe His relationship with us. Something of what I feel as a father is something of what He feels as our Heavenly Father.

Was I harsh and unrelenting when I was teaching my son to walk? No. Did Camden's constant falling incur my wrath and condemnation when he first attempted to walk? Of course not. Do I dwell on my son's failures and weaknesses when I think of my son now? By no means. When Camden began walking, I was patient. At first he fell frequently, but I understood that learning to walk is a progression. I didn't scream, "Would you stop falling, for heaven's sake! When are you ever going to get this right?" When he first began walking, my son was very slow. Very slow. But I was patient with him, because I understood that learning to walk was a progression. I didn't yell, "Would you hurry up, for crying out loud?" Despite the continual spills and the snail's pace, I was pleased to walk with him. He is my son, and I love him.

Nor is our Heavenly Father harsh, demanding, and unrelenting as He teaches us to walk. Our failures do not make Him love us less. That's why it is called unconditional love. He is patient with us when we fall. He loves us when our pace is slow. God knows that learning to walk with Him is a progression. That is why the psalmist could declare, *For He knows my frame. He remembers that we are dust* (Ps. 103:14).

### WALKING WITH MY FATHER

Each summer when I was a boy, my family took a vacation to the South Texas coast. We would load the vehicle and leave in the middle of the night. I always wondered why we left at midnight, but now that I have a son of my own, I understand perfectly. Traveling is much easier and much more enjoyable for parents when the children sleep in the car on long trips! My brother, sister, and I would cram into the back seat and argue constantly over territory. "Steve is in my space! Diana is thinking about getting my seat!" So now I understand perfectly. Just leave at midnight.

All year I looked forward to the trip. I have always said the reason I anticipated this trip so eagerly and spoke of it so glowingly is because I love the ocean and beach. That statement is only partially correct. What I enjoyed the most about the vacation yet never voiced until now is that I really enjoyed spending time with my father. During a typical day my mother was home with my brother, my sister, and me while my father was at work. He was a businessman who put in many long hours. I wanted to spend time with him. While we were away on vacation, he couldn't go to the office; I knew it. We were seven hours away from his office. I knew, because I counted it up. For one entire week I would have my father's attention and could do things with him. I loved it.

Each vacation week usually included fishing. Sometimes we would fish on a nearby pier. We would fish all day. My father would prepare my fishing pole, carefully bait my hook, and was more interested in my catching a fish than he was in his catching one. I loved it.

On occasion we would go out onto a jetty to fish. The jetty was a long pier made of rocks. Much like a wharf it jutted into the gulf a few-hundred yards so you could fish from it. The jetty would often become slippery as the gulf spray crashed against the rocks. My father would always hold my hand tightly as we walked out onto the jetty. He always ensured that I stayed near him the entire time since the jetty would become slippery and dangerous. I loved being out there. I was near my father.

I recall one time when I thought I would please my Dad by showing him how independent I was becoming. I was only about 6 years old. I insisted that I not hold his hand as we walked out onto the jetty. I was getting bigger and could do more things for myself, I thought. Actually I thought he would be more proud of me for becoming more independent. Now that I'm a father, I realize that in situations such as this one, you prefer your child's dependence on you.

However my father agreed to let me walk on my own without his assistance. He was right beside me but did not hold my hand. For fear of showing weakness I did not want to walk gingerly. So I strutted out across the rocks and made my way out into the ocean. Just a few yards onto the wet, slippery rocks, my feet slipped and went straight up into the air. My immediate thought was, "Boy, this is going to hurt when I land!" But before I hit the rocks, while I was still in mid-air, my father reached out and grabbed my hand and arm. He caught me before I landed. He later said he had anticipated I would fall because of the way I was walking, so he was ready when I slipped. "Maybe you are not as big yet as you thought," he said. "Go ahead and hold my hand this time." So once again I grabbed my father's hand. That was fine with me. I loved it.

My earthly father has now gone to heaven, but my Heavenly Father still delights to spend time with me. I enjoy being near Him. I still encounter slippery places in life that would rival a jetty on the South Texas coast. Holding tightly to His hand as I stay near Him in the dangerous places is still necessary. Yes, at times I still try to prove to my Heavenly Father my independence. I want to show how much I have grown spiritually and what I can accomplish now on my own. But I usually slip; He is there to catch me in mid-air. I some-how believe that my Heavenly Father still desires my depending on Him. So, after my miscues, I once again reach for His hand and begin walking with Him. I love it.


**WALKING WITH GOD**

The average person walks between 7,000 and 8,000 steps per day. Over the course of a year these steps accumulate into an average of two-million steps. Amazingly the average person walks about 115,000 miles during a lifetime![5]

The Bible often speaks about walking. To walk, in biblical days, was analogous to living. Biblical writers used the analogy of walking to describe how a person lived his or her life. Perhaps this is another reason why teaching Camden to walk was important to me. It was a symbolic gesture. Throughout his lifetime I want to teach my son to walk in the ways of God.

The psalmists wrote repeatedly about walking. *Blessed is the man who does not walk in the counsel of the ungodly* (Ps. 1:1). David wrote that the person who could dwell in God's sanctuary was the one whose walk was blameless (Ps. 15:1-2). The sons of Korah, ministers of music, wrote that God would not withhold any good thing from those whose walk is blameless (Ps. 84:11). Ethan wrote that the blessed person will walk in the light of God's presence (Ps. 89:15).

Throughout the entire Old Testament the Israelites were encouraged to walk with God. Moses commanded God's people to walk in all the ways in which God had led them (Deut. 5:33; 10:12; 11:22). When the Eastern tribes returned home, Joshua repeated Moses' command by telling the Israelites to *walk in all His ways and obey His commands* (Josh. 22:5). Isaiah repeatedly encouraged God's people to walk in the light of His presence (Isa. 2:3-5; 30:21; 57:2). Jeremiah commanded the people to *ask where the good way is and walk in it* (Jer. 6:16). God promised to walk with the Israelites as He commanded them to walk with Him. Moses gave the law to God's people and also gave them God's promise that He would *walk among them and be their God* (Lev. 26:12).

Walking in Scripture also implied that you shared a close relationship, or fellowship, with one another. The prophet Amos asked, *Can two walk together unless they are agreed?* (Amos 3:3). Jesus promised, "*Whoever follows Me will never walk in darkness*" (John 8:12). In 1 John we are told that if we are in fellowship with God, then we will walk in the light rather than in darkness (1 John 1:6-7). In fact walking is the essence of what God requires of mankind. Micah told God's people, *He has showed you, O man, what is good and what the Lord requires of you? To act justly, love mercy and walk humbly with your God* (Micah 6:8 KJV).

Just before Jesus died, resurrected, and ascended back to the Father, He taught His disciples about the arrival of the Holy Spirit. He promised that when He left the earth, a Comforter would be sent. The Greek wording Jesus chose to use to describe this Comforter was interesting. The Holy Spirit is called the *Paraclete.* This is a compound word which means literally "to walk alongside of someone." Our Savior wanted to assure believers that, after He was gone, He would continue to walk with them each step of the way through the presence of the Holy Spirit.

God allowed me the special privilege of teaching my son to walk. Now, my desire is to teach him to walk with God. Yet this time my walking is modeled before him and not just instructed to him. When I taught him to take those first few steps as an infant, I simply held him up. Yet from now on I will strive to model my behavior as I teach him to walk with God. He will be following my steps.

One evening after his bath Camden was playing while I cleaned up a messy bathroom. During my cleaning I stepped onto one of our freshly vacuumed throw rugs in the bathroom. You could firmly trace the imprint of my foot in the fresh, clean, gray carpet. For some reason this footprint in the carpet fascinated Boomer. He stopped playing, walked over to the place where I was piling up towels, and stared at the imprint in the carpet. "Look Daddy," he exclaimed, "your foot is in the carpet!" I agreed as I looked over his simple discovery. "I want to put my foot inside your foot." So, very carefully, I picked him up and set him down with his little foot inside of my foot. "Look, Boomer," I exclaimed, "you are walking where Daddy walked!"

Just at that moment God spoke to my spirit again, as He has done so often before. He reminded me that my little boy would be watching my actions and my steps—not only this evening after his bath but in the days ahead. He would indeed walk where I walk and would imitate my actions and attitudes. After I had placed the towels in the washing machine and cleaned up the messy bathroom, I breathed a prayer asking God to help me walk upright, as Scripture says, so I will not lead my son down the wrong path as he follows in my footsteps. I can be assured that my son will be walking in the right direction if he follows my steps when I walk with God each day.

## HOLDING HANDS AND WALKING

As I mentioned earlier, one of the true joys of fatherhood is when my son holds my hand. I first held his little hand when he was in the birthing room at Wichita General Hospital. Just minutes after he was born, early on that Independence Day morning, I gently took his tiny hand and placed it into mine. For years I had wondered what holding the hand of my own child would feel like. It felt as wonderful as I had imagined it would feel. My hands are not overly large, but in those early morning hours at the hospital they seemed huge as I held his tiny hand in mine.

Three years later I still feel just as wonderful when I hold my son's hand. The feeling is awesome when he gets out of the vehicle, we start to cross the street, and he instinctively reaches up to grab my hand. The feeling is one of dependence, relationship, friendship, and pure love. We may not even say anything to each other. We'll just walk hand-in-hand. And his hand still looks so small in mine.

My father was 5-feet, 10-inches tall and weighed about 180 pounds with a slim build. Physically he wasn't the most imposing figure. But when I was a child, my father seemed large to me. In our community he almost seemed larger than life. I heard many people brag on my father. Citizens in our community, as well as in the surrounding area, would make a point to tell me, even when I was a child, how my father had helped them. So early in life I began to believe that he was invincible and thought he was a large man.

To my child's eyes the most impressive feature of my father was his hands. They seemed huge. His hand seemed to engulf mine when I placed mine comfortably inside. When we were in public, my father often placed his arm around me when we ate at a restaurant or attended a ball game. When my father placed his arm around me, I felt protected, secure, and warm. His hand seemed to wrap around my entire life, heart first, when I grabbed onto him and we walked together.

My frame is very similar to that of my father. I am 5-feet, 8-inches tall and weigh 165 pounds with a slim build. Physically I am not the most imposing figure. But in the eyes of Camden I am very large. Just the other day he told me, "Daddy, you are big. I want to drink my juice so I can be as big as you some day." I smiled because I knew the truth. For a moment I remembered how I felt about my father. As I grab my son's hand and walk with him, I, too, want to have the influence on him that my father had on me. I want to influence his walk with Christ.

One night while we lay in bed before he fell asleep, my son grabbed my hand, looked it over and said, "Daddy, you have big hands." He fell asleep that night with his entire hand wrapped around my index finger. I could have stayed just like that forever. As my son slept, I lay quietly praying, "Dear God, thank You that You saw fit to give me a son. I love him so much, Lord. I am a blessed man. And, Father, may I always hold onto Your hand tightly and never let it go as I walk with You. In Jesus' name I pray. Amen."

# Chapter 9

# My Son as a Sinner

In 1873 French novelist Victor Hugo began writing the classic work entitled *Ninety Three*. The novel depicted the ravages of the French Revolution after the decapitation of Louis XVI which, as the title alludes, occurred in 1793. Yet the work reflects a deeper conflict couched within Hugo himself and the torment of every soul. In fact one character of the story inspired the tragic exploits of Joseph Stalin in the following years.

In this epic work a ship was caught in a terrible storm during one captivating scene. The crew's fate was endangered by the violent waves but also by the realization that a cannon had been loosed from the deck. Each wave turned the unchained cannon into a battering ram. Finally two soldiers risked their lives to go below and secure the loose cannon. On their descent into the ship they discussed the fact that the cannon within the ship was much more dangerous than was the storm outside.[1]

This image captures the plight of the human soul. Something loosed within each person is destructive. It is called the sinful nature. Often the sinful nature within us poses a much greater danger than does the degradation of the society around us. I had to face the stark realization that my sweet, innocent little boy is a sinner.

## WE DIDN'T TEACH HIM THIS!

We couldn't believe how quickly it happened. We knew it was going to occur, but we were shocked at how soon. Our son's sin nature emerged. Temper tantrums, defiance, outright disobedience, doing the exact opposite of what we wanted him to do—all of these very quickly were a part of Camden's life. When he was only a few months old, we could already see defiance and the beginning of a small temper. In fact after only a few months we could see selfishness appearing in him. Galatians 2:17 states that clearly we are all sinners. Was this verse everpresent early in our home!

We did not teach our son to be a sinner. We did not sit down and show him how to disobey and be selfish. We never instructed him how to be defiant. Obviously we would never do such a thing. Jesus warned about those persons who teach children to sin (Matt. 18:6). But why did Camden seem to know to do wrong? He didn't see defiance and evil modeled in us. Nor was it a learned behavior. We did not sit down with him and teach him, step by step, how to be a sinful boy. Then where did he learn it? Is the sin nature something innate within each of us that simply cannot be suppressed?

From the very beginning we were very careful to present the most positive environment for our son. From early in Camden's life Lisa and I would read Scripture passages to him, pray with him, sing Christian praise songs and great hymns of the faith, tell him how much he was loved, play soothing music, avoid violence on television, and avoid places in which vulgarity would be used. Name anything positive and good; we surrounded him with it. He could not have had a more positive, wholesome environment in which to be reared. Yet very early in his life here was our son acting badly. It made us scratch our heads.

One of the most difficult areas of obedience for Camden once he reached 2 years of age was in the area of sharing. He would horde his toys and other possessions so other children could not approach them. He would avoid situations in which he might have to share his possessions. Lisa and I taught him extensively about the virtues of sharing. We told him that Jesus wants us to share our belongings. Day after day we modeled sharing before him. Yet still he would not share any of his possessions with anyone.

One time, when Camden had just turned 3-years old, we were lecturing him after yet another selfish episode. After another one of our lectures, he looked thoughtfully at us and said, "I think I'm allergic to sharing." In the face of his sincerity we had difficulty containing our laughter. Where had he heard about allergic reactions? How did he connect them to his inability to share?

The next Sunday the preschool coordinator in our church approached us after class and told us laughingly that Boomer had announced to them that morning that he was allergic to sharing. He must have thought that everyone needed to know this fact. Yes, our son's sin nature was now evident to everyone.

I knew we all have a sin nature. For 10 years in the university and seminary I studied theology in a classroom. I earned a doctorate degree in ministry with an emphasis in theology. As a minister I continued to study theology after my formal training. Altogether I have studied theology in-depth for 27 years. So I knew that we all have a sin nature. I didn't expect Camden to be perfect. But how quickly the nature surfaced, how intense it appeared, and how apparent it was so early caught me by surprise.

# WE GET A CLUE

The best place to go to understand human nature is Scripture. The Bible gives us some insight into what goes on deep within each of us about sin. All the way back to the beginning Cain became so jealous of his brother that he killed him. God told humanity then that *sin is crouching at your door* (Gen. 4:7). Moses warned the Israelites, "*Be sure your sin will find you out*" (Num. 32:23). In both the Old and the New Testaments we are reminded that every person is a sinner (1 Kings 8:46; 1 John 1:10). So before my son was even born, I knew that he would be a sinful child.

God doesn't just dismiss sin or view transgression lightly. He doesn't look at us, realize that each person is a sinner, and simply look the other way. Sin caused the death of His Son. Anything which caused the death of my son would receive my hatred. I love my son that much.

For example I would be devastated and heartbroken if cancer were to invade our ranks and take Camden from us. I would probably devote time, energy, and effort and would work feverishly to eradicate cancer so children and families in the future would not endure such devastation. Sin caused the death of God's only Son. He does not find it acceptable when He sees it present in our lives.

For this reason Jesus spoke serious and harsh words about sin. "*If your hand causes you to sin, cut it off. It is better to enter life maimed than with two hands to go into hell. And if your foot causes you to sin, cut it off. It is better for you to enter life crippled than to have two feet and be thrown into hell. And if your eye causes you to sin, pluck it out. It is better for you to enter the kingdom of God with one eye than to have two eyes and be thrown into hell*" (Mk. 9:43-47). I cannot take sin in my life lightly. I have to deal with it. I'm responsible for teaching my son not to take it lightly either. As he grows I will teach him how to deal with it in his life.

Our sinfulness has serious consequences. Moses instructed God's people in the wilderness that each one of them would die because of their own sinfulness (Deut. 24:16). Jeremiah spoke of personal accountability as he warned the Israelites that everyone would die for his own sins (Jer. 31:30). Twice Ezekiel reminded the captives that *the wicked man will die for his sins*" (Ezek. 3:18; 33:8). Paul told the Romans that the wages of sin is death (Rom. 6:23). One day my son will die physically because he is a sinner.

Yet the good news is that Jesus Christ took our place on the cross so we do not have to be lost eternally. This is the same good news that Camden's daddy proclaims each week and has done so for 27 years. Jesus was incarnated and was sent to earth as the perfect Son of God. For 33 years He lived on this planet. Each day of those years was sinless (Heb. 4:15). He died on the cross in my place as my atonement for sin. I will live forever with God in heaven through faith in Jesus.

Still, sin has serious consequences. Even for a believer our transgressions have powerful consequences. Our sin separates us from fellowship with God (1 John 1:6). Unconfessed sin even hinders our prayers where God will not listen to us (Ps. 66:18). Isaiah stated that God's anger was aroused when His people continued to sin (Isa. 64:5). Sin causes believers to lose the joy of their salvation. As he wrote in Psalm 51 David regretted his sin with Bathsheba. The man after God's own heart recounted how terrible unconfessed sin made him feel as a child of God (Ps. 51:8). He asked God to restore to him the joy of his salvation (Ps. 51:12).

I am thankful that Scripture gives me insight into what is going on with my little boy. He is sinful. We will teach him more, as he grows, about sin and what it does to his fellow-ship with his Creator. We will know what is at work within our child, although he is still too young to understand. The sin nature controls him.

## WAS HE BORN THIS WAY?

Late one afternoon I was lying on the bed watching television, just after our son had turned 3-years old, when Camden walked into the bedroom. He was holding a plastic baseball bat. He looked around the room curiously and then finally asked, "Where is Hootie?" Hootie is our housecat who has been in our home for almost 10 years. I asked, "Why are you looking for Hootie?" He replied, "Because I want to hit her." At least he was honest! I think Hootie sensed imminent danger and was probably hiding under the bed.

Where does he get this mean streak? Is my son a sinner because he sins, or does he sin because he is a sinner? It is the age-old theological question, much like the chicken and the egg. In what condition was my son born? Were we at fault because early in life he showed sinful inclinations? Was he a sinner at birth, or did he choose to sin? As a baby did he have a predisposition to sin?

The Bible states that we all were born in sin. But what exactly does that mean? Does it mean that we were all sinners before we even had a chance? David wrote Psalm 51 after his great sin with Bathsheba. In this psalm he poured out his heart to God as he wrote, *Surely, I was sinful at birth; sinful from the time my mother conceived me* (Ps. 51:5).

I believe that being born into sin means that we are born with a sin nature. We are born with a propensity to commit sin. In 1747 Charles Wesley wrote the words to the beautiful hymn "Love Divine, All Loves Excelling", which John Zundel later put to music The old, beautiful hymn states we have a "bent" toward sinning.[2] But only as we act on this sin nature are we declared sinners. The sin nature can rule over us (Ps. 119:133). The wise Solomon wrote that the cords of sin held him fast (Prov. 5:22).

If you say that every human being is born into this world as a sinner, then you have a real problem with Jesus. We know from Scripture that He was sinless and bore our sins as the perfect sacrifice. Yet he had a physical birth. The writer of Hebrews tells us that He was in all points like us, even tempted as we are, yet without sin (Heb. 4:15). Evidently Jesus had a sin nature at birth but never acted on it. Thus He never sinned. Camden has already blown it! He is a sinner. So are his parents. Yes, he was born with a sin nature and became a sinner when he acted on that nature.

The apostle Paul also gave me some insight into how Camden's sin nature operates. In his letters to the Romans, Galatians, Colossians, and Corinthians the apostle wrote extensively about the sin nature and its characteristics. He declares that we are all controlled by the sinful nature (Rom. 7:5; 18, 25).

Yet a person has the power through the Holy Spirit to live above this evil nature once he or she trusts Jesus Christ by faith for salvation. This is why Paul tells us not to live according to the sinful nature (Rom. 8:4; 8-9; 13). He told the Colossians that whatever belonged to this earthly nature was sinful (Col. 3:5).

Camden's actions are sinful as he gratifies the sinful nature (Rom. 13:14). This is why Paul in the entire sixth chapter of his epistle warned the Galatians not to sow to please the sinful nature. He also told the Colossians to "put off" this sinful nature (Col. 2:11). In other words they were to cast it aside, like laying aside an old garment, and put on the new nature Jesus gave them.

As I mentioned earlier, I have told Camden time and again, "I want you to learn to obey Daddy and Mommy so you can learn to obey God." My great desire is for him to grow up to love God with all of his heart and obey God in all areas of his life. It is plain and simple. He cannot obey his sinful nature and still please God (Rom. 8:8). As he grows older, I'll be teaching him this fact. He was born with a sinful nature, but one day I'll explain to him how Jesus can give him a new nature (2 Cor. 5:17). I cannot wait to explain it to him where he can understand it. One of the great joys I anticipate in the future is being able to share with my son the gospel of Jesus Christ in its entirety.

## MY SON IS A SLAVE

On January 31, 1865, indentured servitude was officially abolished in the United States when President Abraham Lincoln signed the Emancipation Proclamation. Yet here in 2006 my son is a slave. He is enslaved to something within his own body. Right now he is a slave to this sinful nature of which I have been speaking. The nature is the master; he is the servant. His actions are sometimes evil because his master tells him to act evil and he obeys. Signs of disobedience appeared early in my son's life because he is enslaved to the sin nature.

The thought of Camden being enslaved is bothersome to me. But I understand it. This fact is why rearing him in the fear and admonition of the Lord is imperative. This truth is why as he grows I'm responsible for teaching him to understand this process. Hopefully he will be able to realize one day that Jesus Christ can give him an entirely new nature (2 Cor. 5:17).

Jesus was the first in Scripture to actually use the word *slave* to describe sin. In John 8 He was speaking to the Pharisees and some other Jewish leaders about their heritage. Jesus had told His disciples if they held to His teaching, then they were His children indeed—that they would know the truth and it would set them free (John 8:32). They responded that they were Abraham's descendants and had never been enslaved to anyone. Jesus replied, "*I tell you the truth, every-one who sins is a slave to sin*" (John 8:34).

In Romans 5 and 6 Paul expounded on Jesus' analogy of slavery in the context of sin. He explained that sin entered the world through one man, Adam, and that death entered the world through sin (Rom. 5:12). This is why my son will die one day. He is a sinner; sinners die. But Paul further explained that where sin increased, grace increased as well (Rom. 5:20). Praise God because my son is extended immeasurable grace from God as well! For this reason Christians have the strength to count ourselves dead to sin but alive to Christ (Rom. 6:11). Paul informed the Romans Christians that sin was not to be their master. They were no longer under law but were under grace (Rom. 6:14). They were no longer slaves to sin but are now slaves to God (Rom. 6:22).

So Camden has hope. During my theological studies I looked in-depth at the different images theologians set forth about the work of Jesus on the cross. One of the powerful images was that of the slave market. After our first transgres-sion against God, we were, in effect, sold into the slave mar-ket of sin. Jesus entered into the slave market, purchased us (which is what the word *redeemed* means), and set us free. So in Christ we have freedom. In Christ my boy has hope to be set free. I'll continue to teach him these concepts and pray that one day he will trust Jesus by faith himself and be set free. More than anything else I desire this for my son. I want my boy freed. But God has given each of us a free will. God requires him to choose the freedom for himself.

I have no reason to get down on myself as a parent because my son is a sinner and enslaved to sin. God's own children were sinners and slaves as well. From creation they were sinners. God called a people of His very own in order to bring humanity back to Himself. He worked through their history in various ways. He gave them the law, spoke to them through prophets, and inspired them through the writings of their sages. Ultimately God became incarnate and walked among His people in the person of Jesus. He took their place on the cross to bring His people back into fellowship with Himself. This is the story of Jesus. It was His very mission. Jesus said, "*I have come to seek and to save that which is lost*" (Luke 19:10). God's own children were lost and enslaved as well. But Jesus Christ set them free as they trusted Him by faith. So my little sinner certainly has hope.

## CAMDEN AND DISCIPLINE

As his parents we cannot allow Camden's disobedience to simply go unchecked. We couldn't stand his unbridled rebellion! Nor could our housecat, Hootie, tolerate his unbridled rebellion! Camden has to be disciplined. I hurt deeply to have to do so, but he needs correction.

Determining the appropriate form of discipline is much more difficult than I had envisioned while we were still childless. During the 18 years we were barren Lisa and I would often allow nieces and nephews to stay with us for a week at a time. Just by judging from those weeks I knew that as a parent, discipline was important and would be difficult to administer. Yet until I actually became a father, I had no idea how difficult disciplining my son would be.

During the pregnancy Lisa and I had extended conversations about disciplining our child. We agreed on the appropriate forms; we have never wavered. We still agree completely as to our son's discipline. Yet administering it still is difficult.

When he was 2 years of age and younger, we would frequently discipline him with a stern but loving "No." If he was headed toward the VCR to insert a cookie, we would re-direct him and tell him he was not to take such action. This often involved gently picking him up and moving him away from the VCR.

As Camden grew, the discipline changed somewhat. We still told him "No" but would often combine the verbal reprimand with a timeout. Sometimes if the behavior merited, we would place him in his room. We would leave him in his room the same number of minutes that matched his age. We left him in timeout two minutes when he was 2-years old. We left him in timeout three minutes when he was 3-years old.

Our form of discipline changed somewhat after Camden turned 3-years old and his understanding grew. We taught him that his actions had consequences. We told him that he would have privileges taken away if he behaved poorly. "Watching your DVD is a privilege that Mommy and Daddy grant you. We will take your privilege away and not allow you to watch your cartoons if you do not obey us," we would say.

Also, after he turned 3-years old, we ensured that our son knew that we, and not he, set the rules. We explained to him acceptable and unacceptable behavior. He was instructed that he would be punished if his behavior was unacceptable.

Knowing how to administer the proper discipline has been a great challenge of fatherhood. The ministers I interviewed spoke of disciplining their children and how great a challenge it was for them as well. In fact the appropriate discipline of their children was the most frequent answer given when I asked them their opinion of the single-most difficult aspect of parenting. Some of the ministers mentioned about how their discipline changed with each of their children and how the personality of the child affected the type of discipline administered. Disciplining my son turned out to be much tougher than I had expected.

What about spanking? In theory Lisa and I do not oppose spanking. I know some organizations, such as the American Parenthood Association, purports that parents are never to spank under any circumstance. When we were reared, my wife and I were both spanked by our parents. Neither of us believed it was inappropriate or that it damaged us physically or emotionally. We agreed that the manner in which the spanking occurred made all the difference.

Parents are to avoid spanking in anger or trying to inflict harm. They are to never spank a baby. We swatted Camden's hand or bottom only when he was old enough to understand why we were doing so. A huge difference exists between swatting and abuse.

Someone once said that children need two pats to help them to grow—one pat on the back and the other pat somewhat lower. Both pats are designed to encourage children to be all God intends them to become in life. A loving parent learns the appropriate time to administer each pat.[3]

By the same token Lisa and I also discovered that spanking our son was perhaps the least effective method of discipline. As he grew, we used it less frequently. Other forms of discipline, such as taking away privileges, were much more effective with Camden. Perhaps other children respond better to spanking than they do to taking away activities they enjoy.

As far as Camden is concerned, we get his attention much more quickly when we remove privileges.

## DOES GOD DISCIPLINE HIS CHILDREN?

The reason Lisa and I decided to be strict about Camden's discipline is because of what Scripture teaches about the topic. The Bible clearly states that a child's discipline is to be expected and administered lovingly. Discipline is a sign of love (Rev. 3:19). From the time He called them, God disciplined His children. The Israelites repeatedly chose wrong actions; God consistently punished them. Sometimes the punishment was lesser, such as taking away their privileges. At other times His punishment was more severe, such as allowing an invading army to capture their land, pillage their spoils, and even take lives. God wanted His children to know He loved and cared for them; therefore, He disciplined them.

Moses taught the Israelites that God chastised them in order to remind them that He was God and to display His great love to them. He said, *You were shown these things so that you might know that the Lord is God; besides Him there is no other. From heaven He made you hear His voice to discipline you* (Deut. 4:35-36). In fact appropriate discipline is a blessing and protects us from possible tragic consequences. The psalmist wrote, *Blessed is the man you discipline, O Lord; the man you teach from Your law. You grant Him relief from days of trouble* (Ps. 94:12-13).

God told His people during the Assyrian Exile that He would discipline them but would do so justly and appropriately (Jer. 30:11; 46:28). Did the Israelites respond when Jeremiah spoke these words? No. God reminded His prophet, *Yet, they did not listen or pay attention. They were stiff-necked and would not listen or respond to discipline* (Jer. 17:23; 32:33).

Proverbs speaks more about the proper discipline of a child than does any other Old Testament book. Remember who wrote most of these wonderful proverbs? Solomon. Remember his story? God granted this son of David unusual wisdom. Solomon didn't always act on this wisdom and often failed as a leader. What kind of discipline did his father, David, administer? We don't know for certain. However years after he was an adult himself, Solomon spoke frequently about the importance of discipline. Eighteen different times in the book of Proverbs, Solomon used the word *discipline*.

This wise king told us that fools despise discipline (Prov. 1:7). He also counseled us not to despise the Lord's discipline (Prov. 3:11). Having been disciplined by your parents yields benefits. Solomon said, *He who heeds discipline shows the way to life, but whoever ignores correction leads others astray* (Prov. 10:17). He also said, *Whoever loves discipline loves knowledge, but he who hates correction is stupid.* Wow, what a way with words! We forbid Camden from using the word *stupid* because it is so harsh. Yet Solomon bluntly called anyone stupid who hates correction. He exhorts children to *Buy the truth and not sell it. Get wisdom, discipline and understanding* (Prov. 23:23).

Solomon encourages parents to discipline their children. Listen to the wonderful promises given to the parent who will discipline his or her child:

• *Discipline your son, for in that there is hope. Do not be a willing party to his death* (Prov. 19:18).

• *Discipline your son and he will give you peace. He will bring delight to your soul* (Prov. 29:17).

Parents are told to offer a child hope by disciplining him or her. Otherwise the parent might as well be sitting back as a willing party to his or her child's destruction. How often do we see this fulfilled before our eyes in our society today? In addition Solomon promised that a son will give a parent peace through his or her correction. A disciplined child brings delight to the soul of a parent.

The New Testament tells us that God disciplines His children. This discipline is proof of sonship. The writer of Hebrews said, *Endure hardship as discipline; God is treating you as sons. For what son is not disciplined by his father? If you are not disciplined (and everyone undergoes discipline), then you are illegitimate children and not true sons* (Heb. 12:7-8). The author quoted other biblical sources when he stated, *My son, do not make light of the Lord's discipline and do not lose heart when He rebukes you because the Lord disciplines those He loves and He punishes everyone He accepts as a son* (Heb. 12:5-6).

Next the writer used the analogy of a father's discipline of his son to teach us about God's chastening of us. He said that our earthly fathers disciplined us and we respected them for it. How much more should we submit to God's discipline? Our earthly fathers did what they believed was best at the time, but God's correction is always perfect (Heb. 12:9-10). No doubt, discipline is painful. We do not like it, but it is necessary. *No discipline seems pleasant at the time, but painful. Later on, however, it produces a harvest of righteousness and peace for those who have been trained by it* (Heb. 12:11).

My parents always told me when they corrected me that administering discipline hurt them worse than it hurt me. When I was a child, I never believed that statement. In fact even as an adult, I didn't realize how true the statement was. For years I joked about it, but when Camden arrived I realized it was no joking matter. Only after I became a father did I understand the depth of what my parents years earlier had said. It really is true. I hurt much deeper than Camden does when I discipline him. Correcting him pains me deeply, but I know that it must be done. It is for his good. I am doing him no favor to withhold correction from him.

I learned so much about God and His discipline of me by being a father and correcting my son. Perhaps God feels the same when He corrects me. He is the One who used the analogy of an earthly father's discipline and His discipline of us. Disciplining His children, whom He loves much more deeply than do I, must pain the heart of a Father. He knows we need the correction. He loves us too much to withhold it from us. My son needs me to hold him to a standard. And, in love, I must do so.

## THE SOLUTION FOR MY SON'S SINFULNESS

Early on we began telling Camden the good news of the gospel. Even before he could speak or respond, we would tell him how much God loved him. When he was a newborn, I would rock him to sleep and tell him how much Jesus loved him. I would walk around the house with him and whisper to him about God's love. Before we put him to bed at night, we would tell him that Jesus loves him. For three years we have continued this procedure. We still constantly remind Camden that God loves him and has a wonderful plan for his life. We take every teachable moment possible to instruct our son about Jesus. We tell him that God made all of nature. God made Mommy and Daddy and our horses and our cats and our dog. We tell him that God gives us our food that we eat. We tell him that God gives the superheroes their strength. We tell him that every good gift he enjoys comes from God (Jas. 1:17).

My greatest desire for my son is that one day he will grow to love the same God whom we love and serve. I pray that one day he will be convicted of his sinfulness and that conviction will lead him to trust Jesus Christ as his personal Savior and Lord. I will not rush the moment nor try to manipulate it. It must be his personal decision made of his own free will. His decision will mean absolutely nothing if he feels coerced into making it or does so simply to please me. I'll just teach him about Jesus and His great love for him and allow the Holy Spirit to bring conviction to my son in His own time.

But when that time arrives, it will be a very exciting and special moment for me. I have often wondered what leading your own son in a prayer in which he placed saving faith in Jesus Christ as Savior and Lord would be like. Through the years as a pastor I have led many, many children in the prayer of faith. What must leading my own child in that prayer feel like? I still wonder. Perhaps I'll have the privilege of doing just that some day. My greatest desire is that Camden arrives at that point in his life in which he trusts Jesus.

I have also wondered what baptizing my own son will be like. I can only imagine what kind of feeling that must be for a minister. Once again during 27 years of ministry I have baptized many, many children. Yet one day perhaps God will allow me the privilege of baptizing my own son.

Yes, my son is a sinner. He will always be a sinner while he is on this earth. But the good news of the gospel is that a solution exists for the penalty of sin. Jesus has already taken it for us (1 John 4:10). He has already taken the penalty for Camden. If my son will trust Jesus and believe in Him, then he will be given a new nature. I pray for that day to arrive at some point in my son's life.

# Chapter 10

# Keeping Watch

It ranks as one of the most remarkable feats of the American West. The Pony Express was in service from April 1860 to November 1861. Its primary mission was to deliver mail, important messages, and news between St. Joseph, MO, and San Francisco, CA. Relay stations were placed every 10 to 15 miles, which was the distance a horse could run in full gallop. Riders could not weigh more than 110 pounds and had to be changed every 75 to 100 miles. As he approached the relay station, the rider would shout loudly that he was arriving so a quick transfer could occur. The station managers were given very short notices, so they would wait outside with a fresh mount and watch for the incoming riders. As a result the Pony Express became synonymous with watchfulness.[1]

No Pony Express station manager watched more closely and with more detail than did Lisa and I as new parents. We watched over Camden like a hawk brooding over its young. We combined abiding love, constant concern, deep compassion, and a sense of responsibility as new, late-in-life, first-time parents. The degree and depth of our watchfulness as parents also added a new dimension to my view of God. From the very beginning I watched over Camden carefully. In fact, night after night for the first few months after we brought Camden home from the hospital, the routine was the same. I would sleep lightly and wonder whether our son was still breathing in the next room. My mind would race and I would wonder, *What if he has stopped breathing?* So, quietly, I would sneak into his room and check on my son. I would watch through the illumination of a night light to see if his chest would rise and fall again. At times I would catch him in the middle of a breath and I could tell immediately that he was alright. At other times he would be lying still and my heart would sink. I would almost panic until I saw, through my bloodshot eyes, his little chest rise again as it inhaled another breath. At times the interval seemed to be forever; my heart would skip a beat until I saw his stomach moving again. Then, wearily, I would go back to bed once I saw that he was breathing and still lying on his back.

However I still did not rest well once I returned to bed. I would lie awake thinking, *I know I just checked on him, but what if he has stopped breathing now? What if he has turned over onto his stomach and he needs me to turn him over onto his back?* So again I would get up and repeat the same routine. I would then fall asleep and sleep lightly. I almost felt guilty for resting. *I don't need to sleep. I need to be watching my son to make sure he continues breathing,* I thought. Then, I would realize how absurd my thoughts were. I had no way to watch over him all of the time, but I wanted to do just that.

## SUDDEN INFANT DEATH SYNDROME

I'll admit that when Camden was first born, I didn't know much about Sudden Infant Death Syndrome. I had heard of it but didn't know many other details about this heartbreaking condition. I thought how tragic losing a child suddenly while he or she was sleeping would be, but I didn't know much more about SIDS. After my son was born, I became deeply concerned about this tragic syndrome. How absolutely devastated we would be if Camden were to die in his sleep! During those first few weeks I often prayed, "Lord, please watch over our son. Surely after all of these years in which Lisa and I were childless, you wouldn't allow him to die of SIDS, would You? Please, God, watch over him and keep him safe. God, keep him breathing."

Sudden Infant Death Syndrome is frightening. The lack of answers concerning the exact cause adds to the apprehension. It is the leading cause of death among infants between one month and 1-year old. The syndrome takes 2,500 infant lives per year in the United States.[2] The unpredictability of SIDS, in spite of years of research, frightens parents. We were certainly two of them.

Three years before Camden was born, Lisa's niece, Misty McClure, lost a baby to SIDS. Keston Brett McClure was only seven-weeks old when he passed away during the early morning hours of November 1, 2000. It was a tragic death. We attended the funeral in Oklahoma and grieved with our family. After Camden was born, Keston's death stayed on my mind. I wondered whether the syndrome was genetic and whether Camden was at a greater risk of dying of SIDS since his cousin had already done so. I discovered that research was not definitive enough to determine the exact causes, including heredity. Most SIDS deaths occur between two and four months of age and more frequently during cold weather. During his first winter months Camden would be during the peak age of SIDS deaths, so my concern increased. But, again I kept thinking, "Surely God will not allow our son to die after such a miraculous birth, would He?"

Because of our concern, Lisa and I visited about SIDS with Dr. Kenneth Sultemeier, our pediatrician in Wichita Falls. He told us about a monitoring device we could rent. The device triggers an alarm if the child stops breathing. I felt relieved and insisted that we wanted to bring it home with our son from the hospital. However the device was unreliable and cumbersome to use. We had to connect our child to electrodes over his entire body and keep him still while he slept, which is almost impossible. Also, other factors would trigger the alarm on the monitoring device and scare us mercilessly. After a few days we decided the monitoring device was simply impractical to use. We put the device away. I went into Camden's bedroom and prayed, "Dear Lord, I cannot keep a constant watch over my son. I want to, but I can't. I have no way I can prevent him from dying in his sleep. But Lord, you are the Giver and Sustainer of life. I plead with You, please watch over our son and keep him safe as he sleeps." I felt more at peace with prayer than I did the device.

Dr. Sultemeier next gave us several precautionary measures we could take to reduce the risk of our son dying in his sleep. We placed our baby on a firm mattress rather than on a pillow, blanket, or other soft surface. We ensured that he did not get too warm while sleeping and kept the room temperature low. In fact Lisa and I almost froze to death in our home because we set the temperature so low. Of course Lisa did not drink or smoke during pregnancy, she received regular prenatal care, and she breastfed him, which also reduced the chances of Camden dying unexpectedly while he slept. We followed the instructions to the letter. But for the very first time I also became aware that our child really belongs to God first. I am certain I will understand this fact even more fully when Camden becomes a teen and then goes off to college. We can watch over him and care for him only so much. We cannot give him his next breath and allow him to continue breathing. Our Heavenly Father graciously allowed us to bear him, but first and foremost he is God's creation.

## GOD KEEPS WATCH

My experience of continually watching over my son, but feeling helpless, increased my awareness of and thankfulness for God's omnipresence. In many theology classes years previous I had studied about His everpresence. After my son's birth the fact that God is everywhere, all-seeing, and that He watches over us sprang alive to me. I noticed more carefully how Christians valued God's watchfulness. I knew it was real but had never valued it as highly as I do so now.

In Genesis 32 Jacob discovered that his brother, Esau, was arriving to meet him. This was their first meeting since Jacob deceived his brother and stole his birthright. Esau had vowed to kill his brother. Jacob did not know what this meeting would hold. God had already promised Jacob that He would be with the patriarch wherever he went (Gen. 28:15). Jacob vowed to the Lord after his enlightening dream at Bethel, "*If God will be with me and will watch over me on this journey I am taking and will give me food to eat and clothes to wear so that I return safely to my father's house, then the Lord will be my God*" (Gen. 28:20-21). Later Jacob's father-in-law, Laban, prayed that God would watch over Jacob and himself while they were away (Gen. 31:49). These servants of God knew very well the importance of God 's watchfulness.

The psalmists were well aware of God's watchful eye and sought His protection as well. In his contrite confession after his sin with Bathsheba, David claimed God's promise, *I will instruct you and teach you in the way you should go; I will counsel you and watch over you* (Ps. 32:8). In Psalm 66:7 the psalmist noted that God's eyes watch continually over the nations. In a psalm the Israelites used in their pilgrimages, God's people sang, *The Lord watches over you—The Lord is your shade at your right hand; the sun will not harm you by day, nor the moon by night. The Lord will keep you from all harm—he will watch over your life* (Ps. 121:5-6).

The Israelites were assured of God's watchfulness when, later in their history, they needed it desperately. After the captives were carried away to Assyria, Isaiah gave them assurance by calling them a fruitful vine which God cares for gently. *I, the Lord, watch over it (the vine). I water it continually. I guard it day and night* (Isa. 27:3). God promised the exiles from Judah that after the Babylonian captivity He would bring them back to their homeland. The Lord promised, *"My eyes will watch over them for their good, and I will bring them back to this land"* (Jer. 24:6). Later He spoke through Jeremiah and told them, *He who scattered Israel will gather them and will watch over His flock like a shepherd* (Jer. 31:10).

I realized that I simply had to trust God to watch over my son. Moreover I realized that I needed Him to watch over me as well. We all—Lisa, Camden, and I—needed God's watchfulness. None of us is capable of taking care of ourselves totally. We all are children in need.

When a child dies from SIDS, that doesn't mean that God failed to keep a vigilant watch over that child. He has a purpose and plan for each of us. Sometimes that plan involves a longer life than at other times. My prayer was for God to use our son's life in length, but whatever He desired was our greatest desire as well. We want God to be glorified, as Paul said, whether by life or death (Phil. 1:20). However we preferred life; we prayed to that end.

## CAUTION: DANGER AHEAD

I am constantly watching out for Camden. I feel it is my responsibility as a parent to watch out for him and ensure that

I keep him out of danger. Lisa and I are both adults and watch out for each other but not to the degree we watch out for our son. He is young, curious, playful, and oblivious to potential danger. Therefore we are responsible for him; we constantly feel the weight of it.

Danger lurks all around a little boy. He is simply unaware of it. If we allow him to do so, Camden will play in a parking lot or street. He will play near water, holes, heights, and many other dangerous places. He will approach animals which could harm him. He will walk in front of moving vehicles, bats and balls, and other children.

Only as we become older do we understand that we can be injured or killed in these settings. But how do you explain this to a small child? You simply have to watch out for danger for children. They don't know any better. We try to explain to him about these dangers, but he doesn't understand. No matter how often we warn him, he is oblivious to the danger around him.

When we cross a street, we always go through the same routine with our son. "Now remember, crossing the street can be dangerous. Take Mommy or Daddy's hand and look both ways before you cross the street." The routine is the same when we are in parking areas. "Son, the cars in this parking area could hit and hurt you. Take Mommy or Daddy's hand and watch out for the cars." He is unaware of the danger, but I am not. As a loving, caring, and responsible father, I watch out for my son and protect him.

When Camden was only 15-months old, I became the senior pastor of the First Baptist Church in Garland. We moved from Iowa Park, where we lived in a parsonage. We child-proofed our home in Iowa Park to where the potential dangers to our son were minimal. We felt secure in letting him play in the parsonage or in our yard.

When we moved to Garland, we purchased a home with three acres on Lake Ray Hubbard; the potential dangers increased. Brick steps lead down into our formal living area. I could envision his running, tripping, and falling headlong into the bricks. Just after we moved, we even made a "dry run" to the nearest hospital so we would know exactly how long medical assistance for his upcoming emergency would take. In only a matter of time this would happen, we were convinced. The house had hardwood floors throughout; this made for much harder landings than had our carpeted floors in Iowa Park. We also now had a flight of stairs, again with hardwood-floor steps, which were potential dangers for a small child.

But my greatest fear for him was outside of our new home. Living on the lake increases the likelihood of creatures crawling into your yard. I know that snakes are a part of God's creation, but I don't like them! When we bought the home, we were warned that poisonous snakes were prevalent in our area. The Cottonmouth Water Moccasin is a dangerous, poisonous water snake. It hides under rocks, limbs, logs, or any other object which provides shade and protection. It will not only stand its ground against perceived danger but will actually aggressively attack. I could envision our curious son simply playing in his yard, uncovering such a snake, and unknowingly approaching it.

Because of these lurking dangers we have taken steps to keep our son safe. We have three cats and one dog, which help keep the snake population down around our home. Also we purchased a snakebite kit and placed it in a prominent place in our house. When we are outside, we watch him constantly and walk beside him most of the time when he is playing. He is unaware of our increased protection and watchfulness. But the eyes of protective parents are always on him.

Camden has grown tired of hearing our constant warnings about dangers. (I know—overprotective, late-in-life, first-time parents!) In fact he has even become angry with me when I try to keep him from danger. He will be so engrossed in a game that he will be oblivious to an approaching car. He will begin to run toward the street and we will grab him. He became angry because he was focused on his interests, his fun, or his game; we interrupted his fun. He was not aware that we were acting for his own good and safety. He was simply upset because we hindered his fun, but we saw the bigger picture.

## GOD PROTECTS HIS CHILDREN

I didn't take long to draw the parallel between my watching out for Camden and God's watching out for me. I learned quickly what God was teaching me about Himself. God watches over me constantly—much like when I watch over my son. I feel frustrated when I cannot look out for my little boy all of the time. Yet God watches over me constantly. His eyes are always on me. *Behold, He who watches over Israel will neither slumber nor sleep* (Ps. 121:4).

Much like Camden is, I am often oblivious to the dangers which lurk around me. I simply am unaware of all of the potential dangers which daily threaten my path. My understanding is limited, but God's understanding is limitless. He sees the bigger picture while I am simply focused on my own world.

Scripture teaches that spiritual warfare is a very present reality. The apostle Paul reminded Christians in the Ephesus region, *For our struggle is not against flesh and blood, but against the rulers, against the authorities, against the power of this dark world and against the spiritual forces of evil in the heavenly realms* (Eph. 6:12).

Yet how does God explain to me all that is taking place around me in the spiritual realm? My understanding is far too limited to comprehend the depth and gravity of many of my situations. If He tried to explain them to me, I do not have the ability to understand. *His thoughts are not my thoughts and his ways are not my ways. As the heavens are much higher than the earth, so God's thoughts are much higher than my thoughts* (Isa. 55:8-9). Thankfully my Heavenly Father is always watching out for me.

Does God increase his protection over me at certain times more than at other times? On occasion does God watch over me as I watch over Camden when he is playing in our yard and I am watching keenly for snakes? In many different ways today's family is under attack by the evil one. Does God protect us from such attacks and we are simply unaware of it? I am often on the front line of Satan's missiles, since I am the primary spiritual leader of the First Baptist Church of Garland. The evil one shoots for the top. He knows that if he can make the leaders fall, then others will fall as well. Does God watch out for me especially while I am unaware of His increased divine protection?

Many times I have heard God speak to my spirit when I have been in our yard, walking beside my son while he plays, and keeping a vigilant watch for danger. Again, it is not in an audible voice but in that still, small voice which whispers, "Greg, I am watching over you just as diligently as you are watching over your son. I love you even more than you love your son. I will always walk beside you." This has happened time and again. God lets me know that He is the responsible Father and I am often the oblivious, playful child. He assures me that His protective eyes are always on me as He walks beside me. I am often reminded of what David wrote, *As the mountains surround Jerusalem, so the Lord surrounds His people* (Ps. 125:2).

In fact God spoke to His own children quite often about His protection of them. God told Moses that He would place him in the cleft of the rock and cover him with His hand (Ex. 33:22). Jesus asked His Father to protect His children by the power of His name (John 17:11). Peter invited all believers to *cast your anxiety on the Lord, for He cares for you* (1 Pet. 5:7). When David was fleeing for his life from Saul, he declared, *I will take refuge in the shadow of your wings until the disaster has passed* (Ps. 57:1). David later testified, *He will cover you with his feathers and under his wings you will find refuge* (Ps. 91:4). The psalmist praised God because He was a *shelter from the storm and a shade from the heat* (Ps. 25:4). During Camden's first three years of life, time and again, Lisa and I have shaded our little boy from the scorching Texas heat. We have shaded, cooled, fanned, and comforted him. How reassuring to know our Heavenly Father offers such wonderful, divine protection of us.

And, yes, much like my son, at times I grow tired of God's constant warnings to me. At moments I even became somewhat angry with the Lord. Although I do not verbalize the words, I sometimes will think them in my heart: *I know, I know, Lord. I need to be more watchful in this area of my life and more diligent in that area.* Like a playful child engrossed in his own interests, I often go through life unaware of what the evil one desires to do to me, my family, and my ministry. I am so thankful that my Heavenly Father watches over me constantly and protects me for my own good. A loving Father does just that.

## "WATCH IT WITH ME!"

Camden is constantly doing things and saying phrases which make Lisa and me laugh! I had always heard how awful the "terrible twos" are. But we also didn't know how much fun having a 2-year-old in our home would be. Yes, at moments the tantrums and defiance emerge in him. But other moments are both precious and priceless.

Our son loves to watch cartoons on his personal, portable DVD player. Mickey Mouse and Donald Duck are two of his favorites. But portions of the cartoon frighten him. I admit, I had never considered Mickey Mouse and Donald Duck as horror flicks, but at times during them Camden is certainly terrified. He becomes frightened and covers his head with the sheets when someone is being chased or an animal chases another animal. He will yell to Lisa or me, "Mommy! Daddy! Hurry! Come here! Watch it with me!" He can't pronounce an "s" very well, so he will say, "This part is cherry!"

At first I didn't understand why he wanted us to watch the cartoon with him. I thought perhaps portions of the animation were his favorites and that he wanted us to share those moments with him. Then I realized that he only wanted us to watch the frightening portions of the cartoon with him. These events were minor to us, but they were very real to him. He wanted us to see the same things he was seeing. Somehow he took comfort in the fact that we were watching what he was watching.

I found interesting the fact that during his anxiety, he didn't want us to hold him. He simply wanted us to watch it with him. He found comfort, not necessarily in our touch, but in our presence. He simply wanted us there. He felt secure when we shared the experience with him. In his little mind if we watched the same events unfolding that he was watching, then he felt protected from any danger. So at times when we are driving down the road with Camden behind us in his child's seat, he yells, "Watch it with me!" We will have to turn the DVD player where we can glance at it while we are driving so he will feel secure in the fact that we are sharing it with him. He feels secure as long as he knows we are near and watching it with him.

Often as parents we have laughed about this scenario. Lisa and I will chuckle when he wants us to watch the "cherry" part of the cartoon. But I guess it is all relative. As an adult some scenarios in life frighten me. The events are nothing to an omnipotent God, but they are scary to me. In my own ways I cry out to God and ask Him to be with me. Just to know His presence is near me and that He is aware of what is unfolding before me makes all the difference. I want to know that God is seeing the same things that I am seeing. I want to be secure that God sees my experiences.

I'm not the only adult who has felt this way. Throughout Scripture God's people felt similar feelings. The psalmist said, *But as for me, it is good to be near God. I have made the Sovereign Lord my refuge* (Ps. 73:28). Again, he declared, *The Lord is near to all who call on Him, to all who call on Him in truth* (Ps. 145:18). David cried out for God not to withdraw His presence from him after Nathan confronted the king about his sin (Ps. 51:11). To the exiles in captivity Jeremiah described God as nearby and not far away (Jer. 23:23). They just wanted to know that God was aware of their situation.

I realized that deep inside each of us is a 2-year-old watching a frightening cartoon. At times each of us desires to cry out to God to be near us. The circumstances are different, but they are equally as frightening to us as an animated character is to my son. Cancer. Death. Divorce. Financial difficulties.

God assures us of His presence, just as I would never turn away my son when he is fearful. We can have great comfort in this fact. God told the Israelites, *"My Presence will go with you and I will give you rest"* (Ex. 33:14). Later He reassured them, "Don't be afraid. I'll be with you" (Deut. 20:1). When they faced one "cherry" situation after another, their loving Heavenly Father comforted His people. *"When you pass through the waters, I will be with you; and when you pass through the rivers, they will not sweep over you. When you walk through the fire, you will not be burned; the flames will not set you ablaze"* (Isa. 43:2). So the next time, I hear my son yelling in a nearby room to come watch the "cherry" part with him, I will look up and thank my Heavenly Father for His continual, abiding presence with me.

## WHEN BAD IS ALLOWED FOR GOOD

I will always recall the day vividly. Camden was only a few months old; the time had arrived for a round of immunization shots. Lisa and I dreaded the day. We would have a difficult time sitting back and watching him hurt. He had a few shots in the hospital at his birth. The nurse swiftly injected him as if this were all in a day's work. He cried and I hurt for him, but he was crying a lot then, so I didn't feel his pain as sharply. But the next round of shots when he was a few months old was a difficult time for us. We held our son constantly for the first few months of his life and had become very attached to him. So this round of shots was probably going to hurt us more than him. We wanted him to know that we loved him and that he could trust us. The thought of holding him while something from the outside caused him pain made us cringe.

We scheduled the appointment with Dr. Sultemeier and circled the date on our kitchen calendar. As it approached, we dreaded the day. The day arrived: we dressed him, buckled him in his car seat, and drove to the doctor's office in Wichita Falls. He didn't know what was about to happen, but we did. As we drove into the clinic parking lot, he was in a jovial mood. This hurt our hearts even more. Our poor little boy didn't know the pain he was about to feel.

We waited with trepidation in the family area of the pediatrician's office until they called our name. All the while we played with our jovial son. Finally the short, blond-haired receptionist called our names. We proceeded back to the exam room. My heart sank. I had butterflies in my stomach. Each Sunday I could preach before hundreds of people in our congregation, but this was tough! Why was I feeling this way? These shots were for his good. The chances of our son contracting deadly diseases would be minimized because of these immunizations. I should be rejoicing that the immunizations are available for him! But I knew the injections would hurt him. They would hurt only temporarily but hurt nonetheless; we would hurt because he hurt.

For a brief, fleeting moment on our way to the exam room, my mind flashed back. Way back—almost 4,000 years. For a brief moment I wondered what was required for Abraham to be obedient to God and to climb Mount Moriah with his son. You see, God had commanded Abraham to sacrifice Isaac (yes, for whom our son was named) as an offering to God (Gen. 22:1).

God allowed a ram to be substituted for Isaac, but think of the agony Abraham must have experienced on the walk toward the appointed place! Then my mind briefly raced ahead 2,000 years—from Abraham's experience to Calvary. Imagine what God the Father must have been feeling as the cross awaited His Son! For a parent to sit back and watch his or her child hurt is difficult.

I held Camden in my arms while the nurse prepared the immunization. This was going to hurt his mother and me more than it would hurt him, so we braced and cringed. Only his leg would hurt. Our hearts would hurt. His upbeat mood quickly turned sour as the nurse gave him three shots. He let out a wail and cried heartily. My heart sank. He looked at me with huge tears in his eyes. I felt as if a dagger was plunged into me. I reasoned that since I was holding him, he could easily associate the pain with me. I hurt to think that my son may associate me with his pain and pull away from me for a while. I kept reminding myself that this awful experience was actually for his good. Lisa and I allowed the nurse to hurt our son momentarily in order to save him from potential pain, suffering, and possibly death later. We were still watching out for him, although he felt pain.

At times God allows painful situations into our lives. We don't understand why and often assume that God is unloving and cannot be trusted. Yet what we do not always see is the reason why bad things are allowed into our life. Quite possibly our loving Heavenly Father is sparing us from worse pain, suffering, or possibly death later. The apostle Paul reminded the Romans, *And we know that in all things God works for the good of those who love Him, who have been called according to His purpose* (Rom. 8:28).

Although they may experience pain, God still watches out for His children. I'm sure that as a Father, He feels pain to see His children hurting. And as His children, we can trust His heart in the midst of the hurt. Just because adversity is allowed into our lives does not mean that God has failed to watch over us. Adversity may actually be the avenue God uses to bring us greater good. If we try to understand the purpose of each single injection, we may possibly miss the greater purpose of the immunization.

## WHEN OUR SON IS ILL

The time I feel most responsible as a father is when my son is ill. This may take the form of a common cold, a virus, the flu, congestion, or another ailment, but Lisa and I will grow concerned about our child. As a parent, holding his little body while it is burning with fever is not a good feeling. I'd much rather be holding him when he feels good and we are playing. Yet I recognize my great responsibility of holding him and taking care of him when he cannot take care of himself.

When our son is ill, the late-night and early morning hours are the worst times as a parent. Camden usually doesn't sleep well when he is sick; therefore, we usually don't sleep well either. His fever usually spikes during the early-morning hours. Many evenings Lisa and I have climbed out of bed and held his little body as it burned with fever. In the early morning hours of illness we have called friends who are in the medical field, contemplated emergency-room visits, prayed frequently, and read instruction labels on medications.

For Lisa and me the routine is usually similar on such evenings. We will determine the medications we can give him and if we are able to alternate any of these safely. We will calculate when he can have these medications and how frequently. We will get cool washcloths for his fevered brow. Then we will lie down to rest for a while ourselves. But the rest on these evenings is not usually very refreshing to us. We will sleep lightly and get up often to check on our son. We will touch his forehead and cheeks to try to estimate his temperature. If he seems to be sleeping and his fever seems to be at a reasonable level, with a sense of relief we will lie back down again for a few minutes and repeat the process again.

Such evenings are not enjoyable to me. But in these early morning hours I feel my responsibilities as Camden's father increase. He needs me; I want to be there. For some reason the day after these restless hours is tolerable for me. I don't feel nearly as tired from the lack of rest that I feel at other times. I wondered why. Perhaps the reason goes back to my feeling of heightened responsibility. I am keeping watch over my son when he is helpless. This is my job as his father.

On many occasions Scripture records instances in which God watched over His children vigilantly. As a loving Father does, He cared for them when they were helpless. King Amaziah of Judah was reminded that when he was powerless, God was his helper (2 Chron. 25:8). David often was in situations in which he felt as if he had no strength. In Psalm 28 he reflected, *The Lord is my strength and my shield. My heart trusts in Him and I am helped* (Psalm 28:7). On another occasion he praised God for being his Help and Deliverer (Ps. 40:17). Through Jeremiah God told the Israelites that they were to simply rely on the Lord's strength. *"So do not fear, for I am with you. Do not be dismayed for I am your God. I will strengthen you and help you. I will uphold you with my righteous right hand"* (Isa. 41:10). The writer of Hebrews said that we can declare with confidence, *The Lord is my helper! I will not be afraid* (Heb. 13:6).

During many evenings of rocking, holding, and caring for my son when he was ill, I was reminded of my Heavenly Father's perfect care. In quiet, still evenings, with crickets chirping outside, I have contemplated my relationship with God and compared it to that of my relationship with my boy. I don't know if Camden will ever grow up to thank Lisa and me for watching over him so lovingly during those nights he was ill. He may thank us one day, or he may not. But I don't want to be guilty of being ungrateful for the tremendous care with which my Heavenly Father watches me. So I have prayed many times during those quiet, still nights and thanked God for watching over me as carefully as He does. Watching over His children is what God does as a loving Father. We are without strength and helpless. We cannot help ourselves. And He is always there . . . keeping watch.

Camden enjoys playing in his cave. He likes to pull the sheets over all three of us as Lisa, Camden and I lie in bed. He calls the resulting tent his cave. As my son and I were lying down one afternoon for a nap, he wanted to lie in his cave. I agreed as long as he lay still. My son lay still for several minutes; then I noticed the sheets rustling. His small body appeared out of the linen, his little head popped out, and he said, "Daddy, is anyone going to get me while I sleep?" As vigorously as I knew how, I assured him that no one would harm him in any way. "Son, Daddy is going to be right here beside you. He will not allow anyone or anything to hurt you. You can rest well." The episode warmed my heart. My son wanted to be assured that I was there and watching over him while he slept. Of course I was overjoyed to let him know of my care and watchfulness. A loving father can do no less.

## THE FINAL WATCH

Only four days after Camden's third birthday Lisa and I toured Greece and Turkey for 10 days with 35 church members and friends. The wonderful excursion traced the Apostle Paul's Second Missionary Journey. This was the longest duration in which we had ever left Camden in the care of someone else. He stayed with some friends with whom he felt very comfortable. He stays with them frequently, keeps "his" toys in their house, and feels at home there. So we were somewhat relieved that Camden would feel at home with his belongings while we were away.

On our return we were eager to see him and highly anticipated our meeting again. Finally the day arrived; we eagerly counted the hours until we would see him. We were all excited as our vehicle rolled to a stop and we saw our beloved son again! I think he made the 10 days better than we did. Although he enjoyed his stay, he was ready to get back to his home. We were ready for him to be with us.

Only one month later I took him to our friend's home for another brief visit. As we traveled there, Camden asked, "Daddy, are you going to stay with me?" "No," I said, "not this time. I will leave for a short while. We will come back to get you." As I drove, I turned around to look at him and saw a saddened countenance. Perhaps he thought we were going to leave him for another 10-day trip. So immediately I began to ponder how I could explain to him that we would not be gone for an extended period. "Son, you will stay for just a few days, but we will not be gone as long as the last time you were here to visit."

Then it occurred to me that the mind of a 3-year-old could not grasp the concept of time. So I used the word *soon*. "Son, I'll not be gone long this time. I'll be back to get you soon." "Soon?" he questioned. "Yes, son, I'll be back to get you soon. We'll go back home and be together again. So play and have fun while I am away, but know that I will return again soon to get you." I wanted my child to continue to enjoy each day but to remember the promise that I'd be back to get him soon.

Camden agreed and did not cry or whimper. He seemed to understand my explanation. At least he made me believe that he understood. He got out of the vehicle when we arrived, kissed me goodbye, and left.

As my friends drove away with Camden, my mind went back to a similar scene. Jesus was about to leave His children and ascend to heaven. They questioned when He would set up the final heavenly kingdom. Jesus responded by telling them that He would be gone for a short while but would return to get them. Since they possessed limited and finite spiritual understanding, the disciples could not comprehend exactly when He would return. So Jesus simply used the word "*soon*." Jesus told His followers that He would not be gone long. He told them that He would return to get them and that they would live together forever. The disciples were to go on with their activities, enjoy life, and spread His message. They were never to forget His wonderful promise that He would return to get them soon.

Our friends told us that Camden watched for us to return for him. Our final watch for our Father to return and get us continues. But we know He will return. He promised He would.

# Chapter 11

# Questions

In 1944 Isidor Isaac Rabi won the Nobel Prize in physics. He won the prestigious award for his work on the resonance method for recording the magnetic properties of atomic nuclei. After he won the award, a reporter interviewed Rabi and asked him various questions. One question centered on how Rabi became a scientist. He replied, "Each day after school, my mother and I would talk about how the day went and what I learned. She always asked me if I had asked good questions that day. My mother told me repeatedly that asking good questions was the method of learning. So, I must say that asking good questions made me a scientist."[1]

Children have an inquisitive nature. They want to know how and why objects function as they do. As was the case with the decorated scientist, this inquisitive nature can be a positive trait and powerful learning vehicle. I just wasn't aware how many questions my son would ask!

## PLENTY OF THEM!

For my entire life I have heard that children ask many questions. This is the stereotypical characteristic of a small child. I knew this already. So I'm really unsure why the fact that my son asked one question after another took me by such surprise. I was caught like a haymaker out of left field directly to the chin. Wow! Does he ever ask questions! A lot questions! Questions about everything—I mean EVERYTHING.

At first Camden didn't ask that many questions. He had a brief period, just after he began putting sentences together, in which he simply accepted things as they were. But the compliant phase did not last very long. Once he reached about 30-months old, the questions began to emerge fast and furiously. Why is the sky blue? How far is up? Why do we go to church? Where is God? Why can't I go with Mommy? Why does Hootie have fur?

`I vaguely remember being a small child (not as small as Camden now) and asking my mother many questions. I asked them endlessly. I also remember her frustration on many occasions. "Because I said so!" she would blurt. As an older child I remember thinking, "When I have a child, I will never tell him that. I will always take the time to explain answers to his questions." I don't think I could have uttered a statement in my childhood which has turned out to be more false. Now I find myself repeating the same answer my mother gave me. "Boomer, because I said so, that's why!"

For example recently we were getting ready to attend church one Sunday evening. Here is how our dialogue unfolded. I said, "Boomer, let's get ready for church. Time to go." "But why are we going to church?" "Because God wants us to go to church." "But why?" "For many reasons but primarily so we can worship Him. Now, let's get your clothes on." "But why do I have to wear clothes?" (How do you answer that?) "Well, for many reasons, but we don't have time to get into all of the them. Now, let's find a shirt. Here is your orange shirt. You like this shirt. Let's put it on." "But why do I have to wear an orange shirt?" "Which color of shirt would you like to wear?" (I thought I'd ask a question back. It didn't work.) "What color do you want me to wear?" "It doesn't matter. You can wear whatever color shirt you want." "But why?" "Because I'm giving you the freedom to choose the color of shirt you want to wear to church." "But why?" "Because I said so, that's why! Now put your orange shirt on. Let's go to church!" "But why do we go to church?" See what I mean?

As a parent, for your child to constantly question you is frustrating. A child is to be obedient to your commands without questioning you. Well, at least that is how I suppose it works in a perfect world.

Lisa and I are the adults in our home (at least on most occasions). We provide all of the necessities our son will ever need. We provide heat in the winter, cool in the summer, clothes on his back, food on his table, and we surround him with love. As a small child his job is to allow us to provide for him and trust us. We will never let him down. He can simply relax and enjoy life while persons greater than he is provide for all of his needs. But this is not how he operates. He wants to be independent. He questions much of what we do and how we do it.

Our situation is not unique. I guess that if you are a parent reading this book, then you can relate to similar frustrations. The ministers I interviewed for this work mentioned some of the frustrations they experienced with their children. Some of them mentioned the patience that was required to be a parent and how their view of God's patience with them had changed.

One day as I grew impatient and frustrated with Camden's persistent questioning, God dropped a thought into my heart. God is wonderful at dropping me simple reminders such as these at the most opportune times. I don't recall which aspect of my decision-making my son questioned, but I was frustrated by it. "Boomer, don't question everything I say and do. Just obey me." Before the words left my lips, I could sense what God was doing. I was about to eat my words. God seemed to repeat the same phrase to me, His child, that I had just said to my child. "Greg, don't question everything I say and do. Just obey Me." Yes, I have a propensity to wonder why God does things in the fashion He does them. I had been humbled; I knew it. Camden stood looking up at me and knew that He had been corrected. I looked up to heaven knowing I, too, had been corrected. One more time, my eye saw Him.

## A HISTORY OF QUESTIONING

God likely grows frustrated with His children's questions. From the very beginning humanity questioned its Creator. The Israelites questioned why God acted the way He acted. Yet their job was not to question. They simply were to be obedient to His commands. He is God; they were His creation. He provided every necessity of life.

God delivered the Israelites from bondage to the Egyptians. In fact He even did so in grand fashion by parting the Red Sea. Next He led them in a route most advantageous to them. He knew if they went by way of the sea, the warlike region of Philistia would discourage His people. So God led them another way. He brought them to the edge of the land He had promised them at Kadesh-Barnea. But they questioned whether they could possess the new territory. So they sent spies into Canaan and questioned what God had already promised them. As a result of their disobedience the Israelites wandered in the wilderness for 40 years. Yet even then God did not forsake them and provided divine guidance daily. He led through a pillar of cloud and fire. He provided manna daily for them. Unbelievably they questioned again.

God established laws to govern their relationships. But even in the giving of the law, the people questioned God's leader, Moses. They grew impatient with him and fashioned a golden calf to worship. Later God's people desired a king like the other nations had. The Lord explained that He was to be their unquestioned leader, but they questioned His plan and sought a king. God reluctantly allowed Saul to be king over the Israelites. The results were disastrous.

Later in their history, during the days of the United Kingdom, the Israelites questioned God's commands and strayed from their relationship with him. The most egregious display of disobedience occurred in the form of worshiping other gods, especially Baal. God warned His children to repent of this idolatry, or He would have no choice but to send judgment on them. The northern kingdom questioned God's prophets and experienced the destruction of its homeland. What residents survived endured years of captivity in Assyria. God then warned the people of the southern kingdom of Judah that the same fate awaited them if they failed to repent. They, too, questioned God. Babylon invaded, as did the Assyrians. This time, Jerusalem was destroyed, the land was pillaged, many Israelites were killed, and the remnant faced difficult years in captivity in Babylon.

Finally God, in the person of Jesus of Nazareth, lived among the Israelites. He taught, worked miracles, fed the hungry, and ultimately gave His life on the cross for their sins. Yet in historical fashion, the people questioned whether Jesus truly was God in the flesh. He ascended back to heaven with the promise that He would return again some day. The people questioned His statement. Jesus' followers then took up His cause and proclaimed His message throughout their known world. Yet the people questioned whether their message was really from God. In the final book of His revealed Word, Jesus promised to return and usher in the final kingdom. Guess what? People today continue to question whether this will occur. I guess you could say that my son quite naturally and honestly gets his tendency to question. He is another in a long line of those who question.

## A BOOK OF QUESTIONS

It is a poetic masterpiece. Many scholars consider it the oldest book of the Bible. It is primarily a book of questions. It dates all the way back to the land of Uz and a man named Job.

We are introduced to Job in the book that bears his name as Satan gathered in a heavenly council to appear before God. Almost like a proud father God asked the evil one if he had noticed Job on the earth. Job was a prosperous yet godly man. Satan responded by implying that the only reason Job served the Most High was because of the special favors granted to him. So God permitted Satan to test Job by removing his blessings. As a result Job lost his children and possessions yet maintained his integrity before God.

Again the council convened. The Lord asked Satan whether he still noticed Job. Satan replied that if he were allowed to strike Job's personal health, then the great servant would curse God. Permission was granted; the evil one struck Job with a horrible disease.

The questions began. Job was in despair over his losses. His wife asked why he simply didn't curse God and die. Job replied with a powerful question of his own, *"You're talking like a foolish woman! Shall we accept good from God and not trouble?"* (Job 2:10).

For the next 36 chapters of the book Job's so-called friends gathered around him and took turns asking him questions. Eliphaz, Bildad, and Zophar were three of Job's friends who tried to comfort him by coercing a confession of sin from him. Job knew of no reason why the trials occurred. He questioned God Himself. The friends were asking questions; Job was asking questions. Later Elihu, a younger friend of Job's, appeared and asked questions of his own but from a different vantage point. Elihu wondered whether perhaps God had a greater plan for the adversity. Perhaps Job was unaware of the plan; perhaps his sinfulness was not the root cause of his difficulties. The young friend's question paved the way for God to finally speak.

During the entire dialogue of Job with his friends, the Lord had not spoken. But in Chapter 38 of the book God finally spoke. God employed an interesting method to approach this dilemma. He chose to ask questions! Yes, God Almighty, the One whom they had questioned, now had some questions of His own for them. Out of a whirlwind God inquired of Job and his friends. The Lord asked Job's friends, "*Who is this that darkens my counsel with words without knowledge?*" (Job 38:2). God then turned to Job and said, "*Brace yourself like a man. I will question you and you shall answer me*" (Job 38:3). In rapid-fire succession God asked Job one question after another. "*Where were you when I laid the earth's foundation? . . . Who marked off its dimensions? . . . Does the rain have a father? . . . Do you know the laws of the heavens? . . . Who provides food for the raven?*" For four chapters God interrogated Job with one question after another (Job 38-41).

Finally Job responded. During the entire questioning from the Lord he had said nothing. This time Job responded—not with questions but with faith. He admitted that he spoke of things of which he had no knowledge. He declared, "*My ears have heard of you but now my eye sees you*" (Job 42:5). The very basis of the title of this book was born out of questions.

Of this powerful drama I have some questions of my own. I find interesting the fact that God only condemned Job's lack of faith in Him, but He didn't condemn Job's questions. Is questioning acceptable as long as our response is one of faith and confidence in God?

I have always wondered about other questions in the story of Job. Why was God silent for so long? Why did He wait for 36 chapters to speak? Did Job feel as if God had abandoned him? Why didn't God interrupt Job's friends when they spoke evil of Him? Why didn't God simply tell Job about His conversation with Satan? Wouldn't an explanation from God to Job as to why these adversities kept happening be much simpler? Wouldn't an explanation have comforted Job much more? Why did God never offer Job an explanation when He finally spoke? Why did He answer Job with more questions?

We still have many questions about this book of questions. To this day questions continue to resound from the lips of my little boy. Can you truly explain some of these questions? I don't think so.

## WHEN MY EXPLANATIONS JUST WON'T DO

Sometimes my explanations and Camden's understanding are poles apart. Carol Podemski knows how I feel. She took her 5-year-old son to visit his grandparents on the farm. While they were there, she thought they would have a wonderful time if she educated her son on farm life and how she was reared. Carol was pointing out to her son how difficult life was on the farm and the skill required to take care of the animals.

The mother and son entered the cow barn and gazed up at a long, handmade ladder which led to the loft. The mother explained, "Son, that is where grandfather kept the hay to feed the cows." The little boy studied the situation for a few brief moments and then said, "I'll bet it was hard for the cows to climb that ladder!"[2]

Camden often emerges with such gems himself. When he does, this helps me know that my explanations are not always on a level at which he can understand. I try to explain things well to him, but sometimes it simply doesn't happen. Camden will fire one question after another; I'll try my best to offer him explanations, but they often don't connect. Right now our understandings are on a different plane. Earlier you saw this in our dialogue over something as simple as getting dressed for church. This happened again the other day.

"Boomer, come here; time to eat supper." "But why do I have to eat supper?" "Because you need nourishment. The food you eat will make you healthy and strong." "But I'm not hungry. Why do I need to eat?" "You will get hungry before bedtime if you don't eat now. And now is supper time." "But why do I need to eat now?" "Because we eat supper now. Mommy and Daddy are eating supper; you need to eat with us." "But why?" "Because we eat supper as a family. You are a special part of this family." "I am? Why?" "Because God gave you to us. We are thankful to Him. You are a special part of our family. Let's eat." "But why do I need to eat?" "Because I said so; that's why!"

When I try to offer explanations to his questions, his 2-year-old mind cannot comprehend my answers. My explanations only lead to more questions, which often lead us farther from the original question. Getting dressed for church and eating supper are simple activities. Several times each week we engage in both of these activities. He certainly doesn't understand our more complex activities. I won't even try to offer explanations for those.

No matter how well I try to offer an explanation to his questions, he simply doesn't understand. The problem isn't necessarily with my explanation as much as it is with his understanding. One day he will understand perfectly. But he is simply too young now to understand the answers to his own questions. I have to answer him by saying what my mother said to me many years ago: "Because I said so." He simply needs to trust what I tell him and obey me.

I really do know what is best for him. I don't know everything about a child, because I am a late-in-life, first-time parent. But I do know some things. For example I know that he needs to brush his teeth. Recently we had a conversation about this simple activity.

"Boomer, you need to brush your teeth before we go." "But why do I need to brush my teeth?" "So your teeth will be healthy. You can get sick by not brushing your teeth." "Sick? But how?" "Well, your teeth decay and your gums have bacteria that can make you sick. So you need to brush your teeth to keep decay and bacteria away." "But why?" "Well, I just told you why. Didn't you understand?" "No." "Well, just brush your teeth like I said. I know what is best for you. Just obey me." "But why do I need to brush my teeth?" Here we go again!

When my son finally stops asking questions and obeys, I am so proud of him. Occasionally I will tell him to do something. Rather than asking, "But why?" he simply says, "OK." When he says that simple word, my heart beams. When he does so, I always commend him: "Good boy, son. Just obey like Mommy and Daddy tell you."

In my son's constant questioning I see a part of myself. By nature I am very inquisitive as well. I want to know how, when, and why. Yet I am called by God to live by faith, not by explanations. The writer of Hebrews reminds us that without faith, we cannot please God (Heb. 11:6).

I have often wondered why God doesn't explain to me why certain things happen and how other events will work out. Why doesn't He simply tell me what He is doing so I will be more eager to join Him in His work? But in observing my little boy's limited understanding I began to understand why. In relation to God, my understanding is possibly limited. If God tried to explain to me, would I simply not understand? If my Lord went into detail about how the spiritual realm works, would my questions possibly only lead to more questions which would get me farther from where I need to be?

As a human being, I have to face the fact that as long as I am on this earth, I will never understand certain questions. Even if God explained them to me, I couldn't understand many truths. The problem is not His explanation. The problem is my understanding. One day I will understand everything perfectly, but I can't now. Our understandings are simply on a different plane right now. The apostle Paul summarized this fact beautifully when he wrote, *When I was a child, I talked like a child, I thought like a child and I reasoned like a child. When I became a man, I put childish ways behind me. Now we see but a poor reflection. Then we shall see face to face. Now I know in part. Then I shall know fully, even as I am fully known* (2 Cor. 13:11-12).

God knows what is best for me, just as I know what is best for my son. I am limited in my knowledge, but I still know better than Camden what he needs. However God knows perfectly what I need. I simply need to trust and obey Him. At times God probably wants to tell me, "Because I said so, that's why!" And God is probably just as proud of me as I am of my son when He gives me a command and I simply say, "OK." Having a son of my own certainly has given me an entirely different perspective of my obedience to God.

In 1886 John Sammis, an Indiana businessman, was leading music at a revival meeting in Brockton, MA, where the fiery evangelist, Dwight L. Moody, was preaching. During one of the services that week Moody offered a testimonial time in which congregants could stand and testify of how God was working in their lives. One young man, a new convert to the faith, stood to his feet and shared his story. The young, uneducated man concluded his testimony by saying, "I don't know what I'm going to do about my situation. I guess I'll just trust and obey." That one simple phrase, *trust and obey*, kept resounding in the mind of Sammis. He jotted down the phrase on a scratch pad and for the next few days pondered the three words. Sammis later wrote out lyrics centered on the phrase *trust and obey* and gave them to a good friend, Daniel Towner, who set the words to music.[3]

The result was the wonderful old hymn, "Trust and Obey," which to this day we still sing—the same hymn which I sang so often as a boy at the First Baptist Church of Boswell. I have no idea how many times I have sung those words, but I know that the old hymn is true. God knows what is best for me. I don't have all of the answers. God's explanations would be far above my head. I simply trust and obey.

## "THOSE ARE THE RULES"

Boomer has always been a "by-the-book" little boy. From his earliest days he was very detailed in all he did. He would line up all of his toys in order and simply look at them rather than playing with them. Any new toy we purchased for him would immediately fit into his system somehow as soon as we gave it to him. He made the determination of where it would be placed before he even played with it. Finally he would get around to actually playing with the toy and periodically would stop to arrange and then re-arrange it. Lisa and I watched in amazement as the toys would be arranged by color, size, and shape. In fact, right now my son is behind me "playing" with his train set while I write this manuscript in my upstairs study. Well, actually he is placing all of the trains in order and just looking at them.

Not only do his toys have their place, he gives his entire life structure. All of his clothes have purpose. He arranges his clothes in some order that makes sense to him, although we can't determine a pattern. Certain clothes are designated for church—not by us but by him. Other sets of clothes are exclusively for golf, football, basketball, soccer, sleeping, playing, etc. We can never interchange these clothes and use them for anything other than for what he has them designated. Shoes, socks, and underclothes are the same.

As I've already mentioned, when he was 2, Camden became a superhero fan. He loved to watch and re-enact scenes from Batman, Superman, Spiderman, Power Rangers, and Ninja Turtles. Family members would purchase him costumes and items of these superheroes. Rather than playing with them, he would place them all together, stand back, and simply look at them. Even the superhero toothpaste and bandages we bought for him were placed together in a bathroom closet. All were lined up perfectly. From time to time Boomer would open the closet door and simply look at them. Then on occasion he would straighten them so they all were uniform.

Lisa and I often wondered if perhaps our son had OCD (Obsessive-Compulsive Disorder). I am a very detailed, organized person who enjoys structure. So Camden developed this trait naturally. However, when he was only 2, his obsession with structure and order surpassed mine. His obsession is both a blessing and a curse. Having a child who desires structure is a blessing. I hope he still has that same attitude when he becomes a teen! However times occur when we need him to be somewhat more flexible. For example certain clothes may need to be washed, but if he has designated them for a specific activity, then no substituting can occur. He maintains his rigidity and seems to panic if we try to change the rules.

When he learned to talk, our son verbalized his obsessions. Repeatedly he would comment that he always does certain things a certain way. He seemed rather proud of the trait. One of his favorite phrases became, "Those are the rules." All we had to do was tell him, "Those are the rules", if we wanted him to learn something the correct way. He wouldn't say a word but would carry out what we told him to do. From that day forward the activity had to be done in that manner, because "those are the rules." At times Lisa and I would forget and try to do the same, mundane activity differently, but our son would remind us that we had to do it the previous way because "those are the rules." Again I am thankful that we have a son who desires to abide by the rules. Sadly this desire is greater than is his desire to obey his parents, but we use this phrase to our advantage.

Once our son knew the phrase "those are the rules," he didn't ask as many questions. When he would ask me his patented "why" questions, I would simply respond, "Because those are the rules." Once he heard that phrase, he would then proceed to do what we had asked of him and didn't ask as many questions. A standard had been set; he was content. A set standard to which he was to adhere helped ease the number and scope of his questions.

Camden does very well within a fence. Perhaps his obsession with following the rules helps his attitude toward the confinement. Once he turned 3-years old, we allowed him to visit with friends in their homes and play. We would instruct him that he must stay within the fenced backyard and never leave it while they are outside playing. He has no problem with our command. In fact I don't recall once he has ever questioned this command because we always tell him, "That is the rule." Within our own yard we tell him where he can and cannot play and always conclude our imperative with the phrase, "and that is the rule." This is certainly a blessing to his parents, since we don't have to worry about him wandering too far and getting into trouble.

Did God create us in this way? Is Camden's nature innate? Does the fact that God has established an absolute standard for us help our need to question constantly? I still have questions about many things in life, but I know my standard is God's Word. I believe and accept this standard as the sole authority in life. I agree wholeheartedly with *The Baptist Faith and Message* when it states, "Scripture has God as its author, salvation as its end and truth, without mixture of error, for its content."[4] It is the ultimate standard. I must change my beliefs, actions, or attitudes to coincide with those of Scripture. The Bible is our fence—the boundary God has set for us.

I have explained to my son repeatedly that even Mommy and Daddy have rules. I told Camden, "Son, Mommy and Daddy are required to do certain things because God has told us to do them. We must obey God, just as you obey us. God has given us rules, too. They are found in the Bible." Once again he replied, "OK", and walked away. What a great response, even for his Daddy!

### HEARING A VOICE DISPELS THE QUESTIONS

"Mommy, where are you?" "Daddy, are you in there?" We constantly hear these and similar questions in our home. When he is in his room playing, Camden wants to be reassured that his parents are nearby. He will yell out to us; if he hears our voices, then he is all right. He will continue playing by himself. He just needs the reassurance from our voices that we are still near.

From time to time Lisa will go feed the horses or I will take out the garbage. We will go outside the house. Camden will remain inside playing in his room or watching a cartoon. Soon he will call out to see if we are still near. "Mommy, where are you?" "Daddy, are you in there?" While we are outside, we can hear his faint, shrill voice calling us. If we do not answer, he assumes that we are not in the house, so he will open the door and repeat the questions. "Mommy, are you out there?" "Daddy, where are you?"

We will yell back and tell him where we are and what we are doing. Then he will shut the door and continue his activity. As long as his questions are answered with our presence, he is content. Hearing our voices brings him comfort and reassurance.

In Chapter 5 I wrote about the ability to distinguish my son's voice from other voices. The Israelites felt the same way toward God. When He spoke reassuring words to them, His voice brought His children comfort. They knew His voice; it brought comfort.

God's people described God's voice in various ways. Adam and Eve heard the sound of God walking in the Garden and hid (Gen. 3:8). Both Ezekiel and John compared the Lord's voice to the sound of rushing water (Ezek. 34:2; Rev. 1:15). God's audible voice spoke during Jesus' earthly ministry. God's voice boomed approval from heaven at Jesus' baptism (Mt. 3:17). Later in Jesus' ministry, witnesses said that God's voice thundered approval of His divine Son (John 12:28-29). In the parable of the bridegroom Jesus declared that the sound of the Son of Man's voice brought joy to His followers (John 3:29). On the Damascus Road, Saul heard God's voice and recognized it as the voice of Jesus. Saul's life was changed forever (Acts 9:3-4).

Something about hearing their Father's voice still brings comfort to God's children today. My questions and fears are dispelled when I hear God speak and I know that He is nearby.

In the days ahead I'm certain my son will continue to ask questions. Perhaps this trait is inherited from his father. I'm certain that many times I won't have the answers to offer him a satisfying explanation. But as long as I can convince him "those are the rules," then perhaps he will trust my heart and know that I love him and have his best interests in mind. I hope the sound of my voice continues to bring my son comfort and to dispel any fears which may gather in his heart. These are the desires of my heart for my son. When I think about it, these are the same desires I have as a son when I think about my Father.

# Chapter 12

# The Joy in the Journey

Last Sunday morning at church, someone said it to me again. The topic of our little boy entered into in a conversation I was having with an elderly woman in the hallway. She asked how Camden was doing. I shared with her a few, brief incidents. The woman smiled, looked up, and said, "Pastor, you didn't realize how much you were missing all of those years when you didn't have a child, did you?" I returned the smile and said, "No, we really didn't know how much we were missing. He is a lot of fun! He has certainly brought joy to our home."

Before Camden arrived in it, our home was a happy one. But it was different. Lisa and I grew up together in the same small, southeastern Oklahoma town of Boswell. Since our families knew each other, for most of my life I was acquainted with her. During the summer of 1979 I recommitted my life to God and surrendered to His calling on my life into vocational ministry. During that same summer Lisa became a Christian during Youth Camp Week at Falls Creek Baptist Assembly. On Sunday evenings after the worship service the pastor of our home church began a discipleship class for new believers. Of course Lisa was in the class and I wanted to take it also since I had recently surrendered to the ministry. In this class we began to get to know each other better and develop an interest in each other.

Soon after this we began dating and courted for almost three years before we married. During this time period I was serving as pastor of Floyd Baptist Church near Greenville, and attending seminary in Fort Worth. We married on February 1, 1985, in our home church. We had discussed children and wanted to wait a while before we had them. I was working on my master of divinity degree; Lisa accepted a secretary position at a nearby elementary school. We agreed that children needed to wait. We agreed that five years into our marriage would be ideal to begin having children. Little did we know.

Lisa and I are both very independent, so we each were involved in own interests when just the two of us were in our home. We also shared many common interests, so we enjoyed a very good marriage. Our relationship has always been a close one, since we have known each other almost our entire lives. For 18 years we shared many interests and ministry. We had a good life and a good marriage. We had no complaints. We could have continued without a child and had a good life. But the elderly woman was correct. A dimension of our lives was missed. Yet we didn't realize the depth of the void until Camden actually arrived.

Children are a gift from God (Ps. 127). Bearing them is to be viewed as a gift from the Lord, not simply as the choice of parents when the right timing works out. Rearing them is a tremendous responsibility. God must direct you and give you wisdom as you train them in the *nurture and admonition of the Lord* (Eph. 6:4).

When we had that memorable visit to the Italian restaurant in Wichita Falls that I described in the opening chapter, with uncertainty we were staring at each other across the table. We had so many questions but were filled with excitement! We didn't realize how much more complicated our lives would become. But we also didn't realize how much more joy was about to enter our lives, either. Dr. Wendell Estep serves as the senior pastor of the First Baptist Church in Columbia, SC, and is a good friend of mine. When we were informed that we were pregnant, Dr. Estep sent a congratulatory email to me. In the correspondence he said, "Your life is about to become incredibly more complicated but incredibly more blessed." Many times in the three intervening years I have remembered his words. Dr. Estep was exactly on target with his comment. Life with a child is much more complicated but incredibly more blessed!

The ministers interviewed for this book reflected Dr. Estep's sentiment. I asked them, "What surprised you the most about being a first-time father?" Seventy percent of them mentioned either the great joy the child brought to their home or the great responsibility accompanying the blessing. Several ministers mentioned that they had no idea how much of a blessing their child would be to them. Others shared how much more responsibility they felt on their shoulders as a father. One minister replied, "I had no idea how selfish I had been for years before I had children." For three years similar thoughts have filled my mind. Yes, life has become incredibly more complicated but incredibly more blessed!

Camden Isaac has brought so much more joy to an already good marriage and wonderful life. The difference is exponential. Through this little boy I have learned so much more about myself, my father, my upbringing, my life, and, most of all, my Heavenly Father. He has added so much joy to the journey.


## "I WANT TO BE LIKE YOU, DADDY"

I had just had one of those days. You know the kind of day I'm talking about. You have had them, too. The entire day nothing seemed to go right. A lot was on my mind. I had many appointments on the schedule. I was already behind on a couple of projects at the church. I also had the weekly pressure of deadlines which had to be met. Also I had the weekly responsibility of serving as the pastor of a 5,200-member congregation and the time-consuming details that accompany the position. In the midst of it all I was trying to carve out time somewhere to write this manuscript.

The day was a Tuesday, which means a long workday with long hours. Tuesdays often begin for me at 7 a.m. and sometimes conclude around 9 p.m. or later. I hadn't eaten much all day; I was hungry. Hours earlier the lunch burrito I ate at a fast-food restaurant had worn off. Honestly, when I finally arrived home from work, I was somewhat irritable.

I pulled into the driveway at my home, stopped the vehicle, and turned off the engine. The only thing on my mind was what I did not get accomplished that day and how much further behind I felt. I reached to grab the briefcase from my truck as I contemplated how to arrange my schedule the next day so I could catch up on my workload. In the dark I walked toward the house with my mind whirring about Wednesday's schedule the next day.

I opened the door and immediately heard the shrill voice, "Daddy!" My mind left my schedule and instantly went to my son. "Boomer!" I sat my briefcase down, picked him up, and watched joyfully as a huge smile spread across his face. I asked how his day went. We spent some time together reliving what he had done.

After a while I began unloading my briefcase and the cargo I had collected throughout the day. I was still unusually quiet and very tired. Camden watched intently as I went through my nightly routine. I changed clothes and headed for my closet. Little Boomer followed me. When it happened, I was in the closest hanging up clothes with my mind still drifting to my busy schedule.

Camden was standing outside the closet watching me hang up clothes. He was quiet but intent. "Daddy," my son said. "Yes, son," I responded, only about halfway listening. "I want to be like you." I was stunned. He had never said that before. I asked again to make sure I heard what he said. "What did you say, son?" I asked. "I want to be like you, Daddy." I stopped immediately what I was doing. Tears filled my eyes. In fact they fill them again now as I write about the incident. The clothes could wait to be placed onto a hanger. I walked over and picked up my little boy. "I love you, son. And you know what?" "What?" he asked. "In many, many ways I want to be like you." I was being honest with him. I would love to emulate the simple love of life he displays. I also want to show love to my Father that he shows to me.

All of a sudden the long hours of the day didn't affect me any more. The busy, upcoming schedule and projects didn't matter. I didn't notice my fatigue and hunger. In fact I even forgot that I had had one of those dreaded Tuesdays. The moment was a joyful one. My son, in sincerity, looked up at me and simply said that he wants to be like me. My heart melted.

I know many sons have said that phrase to fathers before, but this was a very emotional moment for me. A myriad of thoughts flooded my mind while I stood in the closest looking back at my son, who had just uttered those seven magical words: *I want to be like you, Daddy.* I am well aware of what Dorothy Law Nolte wrote, "If a child lives with criticism, he learns to condemn. If a child lives with hostility, he learns violence. If a child lives with ridicule, he learns to be shy. If a child lives with shame, he learns to feel guilty. But, if a child lives with encouragement, he learns confidence. If a child lives with praise, he learns to appreciate. If a child lives with fairness, he learns justice. If a child lives with approval, he learns to like himself. And if a child lives with acceptance and friendship, he learns to love the world."[1] I am certainly cognizant of the fact that through my example he will learn much about how he relates to the world. He stated that He wants to be like me. What an awesome responsibility!

I thought about how for years I had longed for a child before whom I could model a life. But for many years I was uncertain whether the day would occur. I envisioned a day when a little boy would look up at me and tell me that he wanted to be like me. And now God had graciously given me that day. You see, more than 40 years ago I was that little boy. So vividly I recall watching my father get dressed for work and thinking, "I want to be just like him someday." I looked up to my father. He was intelligent, sharply dressed, always smelled of cologne, and had a certain presence about him. I wanted to be like him. And now here was my little boy watching me and expressing his desire to be like me. (Why can't I stop crying while writing this?)

But in that wonderful moment, a greater thought went through my mind. I envisioned myself standing before my Heavenly Father. I envisioned standing before Him with the same sense of awe, inspiration, and sincerity that my little boy possessed. I want to tell my Father how much I want to be like Him. I truly desire that. I want to emulate God's love, compassion, and forgiveness. I want to be like my Father. In many ways I am not like Him and have so far to go, as we all do. Yet the desire is there. All over again I truly want to be like my Father.

The rest of the night I beamed. Seven simple words from someone whom I love dearly had rejuvenated me. That night before I went to bed, I stayed up longer than usual. A whole new day seemed to have already begun for me. Before I finally retired for the evening, I got alone and thanked God for the day. I thanked Him for His presence, power, and sustenance. And I thanked Him again, as I have so many times before, for my son. What a blessing he is to us! And then, to close a tiring day, I prayed, "Dear God, I love You. And I truly want to be like You."

## WATCHING HIM LAUGH

When a smile begins to crease his face, my son has beautiful dimples. The corners of his mouth turn upward when he begins to smile. At such times he looks a lot like his mother.

Her entire life Lisa has always had a quick smile. In fact when she was a little girl, her family affectionately nicknamed her "Smiley." Camden has his mother's cute smile. His brown eyes, which so much resemble his mother's eyes, sparkle when he grins at you. The expression of his face, when he grins, is truly indescribable, but it a wonderful experience for a father. He has always been quick to grin. He was a happy baby and grinned quickly even when he was just a few weeks old. His grin is memorable and infectious. I cannot help but grin each time he grins. I can't put my finger on it; describing it is almost impossible, but something inside of me happens each time I see my son grin. I didn't think it I would feel the way I do just to see my son smile.

When he laughs, the joy for me is even greater. Something is very special about the laughter of a child. Research shows that a child laughs an average of 400 times a day, compared with only 15 laughs a day for adults. Perhaps adults lose their joy as they grow older.[2] I have the greatest feeling when my little boy laughs until he loses his breath!

One evening Camden and I were wrestling in the floor—another dream for which I had longed for many years. During one of our mock struggles our heads accidentally collided. They banged into each other with a thud. I was concerned that Camden was injured and would raise his head with tears filling his eyes. However just the opposite happened. He was laughing! In fact he was laughing hysterically! Boomer was laughing so hard that he would lose his breath and struggle to catch it again. I don't know why he thought head-banging was so funny. But I got such joy out of seeing him laugh so hard. Of course I re-enacted our heads colliding again, this time without much force. Again he rolled in the floor laughing uncontrollably. Just to watch him laugh I repeated this time and again. What a great joy to see my little boy laugh!

As I have documented throughout this book, many aspects of fatherhood surprised me when I actually experienced them. But one of the greatest and most pleasant surprises was how much I would enjoy seeing my son enjoy himself. I absolutely love times when he is joyful.

Honestly, I had never given much thought to how God views my joy. The image that many people have of God is one of judgment, condemnation, and rigidity. They view Him, not as a delightful God, but One who frowns on anyone on earth enjoying life. They view God as a demanding taskmaster Who can never be pleased. Yet God in His revealed Word describes Himself as a loving Father. However I delight to see my son joyful. Why would God use this analogy of a father to describe Himself if He is serious and stern and doesn't want His children to experience any kind of joy?

I began researching what God, in His Word, said about His children's joy. I was surprised at my findings. Time and again God mentions the delight He experiences when His children are joyful. In Psalm 16 David testified to God, *You have made known to me the path of life. You fill me with joy in Your presence, with eternal pleasures at Your right hand* (Ps. 16:11). Nehemiah led a group of captives back to Jerusalem to rebuild the city walls after they were in exile in Babylon. God didn't want to bring judgment on His people but believed He must. When he did so, his heart hurt. Nehemiah returned with the exiles and reminded them that their joy in the Lord would be their strength (Neh. 8:10).

What does Scripture reveal about Jesus and joy? Many theologians have portrayed the Savior as somber. But the New Testament speaks frequently of His joy. He was full of joy and rejoiced when the Father revealed spiritual truths to babes rather than to the wise and learned (Luke 10:21). Jesus often mentioned that He desired that His followers have the same joy He had. Jesus told His disciples that He gave them the vine and branch analogy so *"that My joy may be in you and that your joy may be complete"* (John 15:11). Only one chapter later the Savior then told His disciples to ask and they'll receive so that their joy would be complete (John 16:24). Another chapter later, Jesus in his beautiful intercessory prayer prayed to the Father that His children would experience the full measure of His joy (John 17:13) Evidently my wish for my son is similar to what Jesus desired for His followers—that my child experience the full measure of joy.

Other biblical writers wrote of the joy God desires that His children enjoy. Authors of the New Testament epistles wrote frequently of joy, although many of the letters were couched in the context of persecution. Paul told the Romans that the qualities of the Kingdom of God are not matters of eating and drinking but of righteousness, peace, and joy (Rom. 14:7). The writer of Hebrews spoke of the joy set before Jesus, which caused Him to be obedient to the Father to the point of a cross (Heb. 12:2). Peter, who failed Jesus terribly at the cross and denied he even knew the Savior, later wrote that believing in Jesus filled him with inexpressible and glorious joy (1 Pet. 1:8). According to tradition Peter was crucified with his head downward.

During His earthly ministry, joy was a primary characteristic of Jesus. After His ascension it was also a prime characteristic of Jesus' followers. I desire it always be a characteristic of my son. A loving father loves to see joyful children.


## BEING SEEN WITH HIM

In the past I rolled my eyes at such doting parents. Now I have become one! Of course I think my son is the cutest child on the planet. I love being seen with him in public. When he was a newborn and we took Camden into public settings, others would stop and comment on the tiny baby. As first-time parents Lisa and I would beam with pride. We simply overlooked questions such as, "Is this your grandbaby?" We were hoping they were noticing how cute our son was rather than how old we were!

As he grew older, we still were so proud of him and wanted to show him off. When we were in a restaurant or business, we loved for people to comment on our "cute" and "well-behaved" child. I felt as though everyone in the business was admiring my son, though I knew that they were not. I was simply so proud of him that my sense of sound reasoning left.

To this day I still love being seen with Camden. I enjoy when he rides on my shoulders and others see us. When he has on his full Spiderman costume, I am filled with pride when we enter a business and everyone in the place dotes on him. Of course at church he is in the public eye constantly, since he is the son of the senior pastor. But as a father I enjoy others noticing and commenting on him.

When we are around family and friends, we tell them "Camden" stories. They ask about him; we go on and on about our son. We try to get him to repeat for them some of the cute phrases which he has said to us. I simply want others to know him better. I want others to know the Camden I know and love so dearly. I want them to get to know the personality that we know so well. I want them to love him more. As a proud father I believe that once they get to know him better, I'm certain they will love him also.

Soon after Camden's birth Lisa and I took a family outing to the Sikes Center Mall in Wichita Falls. As we walked in the mall, I insisted on hoisting the child carrier. For some reason I believed it was my job. I'm sure Lisa was delighted for me to offer. A powerful sense of pride was within me as I carried my son. I would look to see if others were watching. Some mothers watched, but most everyone else was going about his or her shopping. I noticed that I didn't have as much of a desire to go into the sporting goods stores or bookstores as I usually did. I only wanted to be seen with my son and for others to notice him. I knew right away that my priorities had changed and that parental love is different than is any other love I had experienced.

Each Monday I go to the church office about 45 minutes late so I can take Camden with me to Parent's Day Out. Although he is fun and adorable, his mother still needs a break! He stays in the church's day care until 2 p.m. Each Monday this is a special time for me when I get him out of his car seat, take him by the hand, and we walk side by side into the church facility. Church members often will be gathering at the facilities for a number of activities, so they will see us walking across the parking lot toward the nursery door. Many of them will smile and wave while they whisper to a family member or friend. I have no way of telling what they are commenting, but in my mind they are extolling the virtues of my son! I absolutely enjoy that time of walking hand-in-hand with my son and allowing others to see him. During those memorable walks I am most definitely a proud father.

Recently the First Baptist Church of Garland held a preschool and children's program one Sunday evening. As part of the program, preschoolers assembled on the platform and sang two songs. Right in the middle of the children, with a terrified look on his face, was our little boy. Lisa and I sat on the front row, camera in hand, and wanted to enjoy the experience as "old", first-time parents. We laughed as he tried to mimic the motions to a couple of the songs. Of course he was about five seconds behind on each of the motions. We commented to each other on how wonderful he was. I'm sure the other children's parents were saying the same about their children. His portion of the program concluded; the service continued. For the remainder of the service I ushered him to the nursery.

As we left the sanctuary, hand-in-hand, I was so proud of my son—not because his motions were concise and on cue. They were not. Not because his notes were on perfect pitch. They were not. I was proud as we exited the sanctuary simply because he was mine and I loved him with all of my heart. The feeling deep within me was indescribable. It was a feeling of joy . . . completeness . . . well, quite simply, love.

Is this how God feels about us? Does He really love us that much? Is He as proud of us as I am of my son? Does He desire to be with us as much as I do my son? Does He want to walk hand-in-hand with us and close by our side, like I do my son? Really? This fact is difficult to believe, isn't it? According to Scripture my love and affection for Camden is only a slight, imperfect picture of God's amazing love for us. His agape, unconditional love is perfect, which far surpasses my human, imperfect love. God must love us many times over how much I love my son.

Often the Bible tells us how God delights in His children. Moses told the Israelites that God delighted in them (Deut. 30:9). The psalmist said, *For the Lord takes delight in His people* (Ps. 149:4). The biblical writer who wrote of God's love for His people the most frequently was Isaiah. This fact struck me as odd, since through this prophet God had to announce His judgment on Israel. Don't you think that the time when you tell your child how proud you are of him or her would not coincide with the time when the child had sinned greatly?

Yet Isaiah is the book in which God told the Israelites that they were the garden of His delight (Isa. 5:7). The eighth-century prophet reminded them that God still took delight in them (Isa. 62:4; 65:19). Even Jeremiah told the Israelites that God took delight in them (Jer. 31:20). When Jesus was born, the angel told Mary and Joseph that the child would be a delight to them (Luke 1:14).

Why does God love us so much? With one failure after another, day after day, why does He still have such affection for us that He calls us *a delight*? I guess this would compare to my asking why I love Camden so much. Doesn't he disappoint me, disobey my commands, and commit sins? Sure, he does. But these facts do not change my love for him. In the songs of life, we are far from on perfect pitch, but God still loves us. We are far behind on the motions, but God still delights in us. He desires to walk hand-in-hand with us. Why? Simply because we are His and He loves us with all of His heart.

## CARRYING HIM

Throughout our pregnancy I was somewhat apprehensive about holding our new baby when he arrived. I am the youngest of three children. Neither sibling of mine is within five years of me. Needless to say, I was not reared with small children around the house. My entire life I have never been around babies or small children to a great extent. Friends laughed at how awkward I looked when I would be "forced" by a mother to hold her child at church. So you can imagine my apprehension at the prospect of holding, carrying, and taking care of my child. But the moment Camden was born, I had a natural instinct to want to hold him. When I first saw him, the desire was present instantly.

As time went by, holding my son and carrying him became like a second nature to me. I enjoy carrying him. At first he was easy to carry. He was tiny and wrapped in blankets. Later, when he could hold up his head, I carried him differently but still relished the opportunity. Now, he is 3-years old and tall for his age, so at times carrying him is awkward. But I still love to do it. Camden and his parents have a bond because we have carried him so often for so long. He trusts us when we carry him and knows we will not allow him to fall.

I carry my son for different reasons. At times I carry him because he is tired and has little strength. At other times I carry him because we are in a hurry; doing so is faster than is his walking beside us. Sometimes I pick him up simply because he wants me to carry him, although I see no apparent reason. Still other times I carry him because he has fallen asleep in the vehicle and is sleeping soundly when we arrive. Regardless of the reason, I carry him with great love and care. I enjoy each moment I carry him because we have a special bond between us. A part of the joy of my journey is being able to carry my son.

God and His people also had a special connection when He carried them. Quite often God used the analogy of carrying the Israelites. In fact Moses told the Israelites, "(In the desert), *there you saw how the Lord your God carried you, as a father carries his son . . .*" (Deut. 1:31). God told His people that He carried them on His wings as an eagle carries her young and brought them to Himself (Ex. 19:4). He later used the same eagle comparison when the Israelites were in the wilderness (Deut. 32:11). Centuries later God still told the Israelites that He was carrying them, but this time He used the imagery of a flock of sheep. *He tends His flock like a shepherd. He gathers the lambs in His arms and carries them close to His heart. He gently leads those that are young* (Isa. 40:11). Isaiah reminded the Israelites that God would never allow them to fall. "*Even to your old age and gray hairs I am He. I am He who will sustain you. I have made you and I will carry you. I will sustain you and rescue you*" (Isa. 46:4).

God carried His children for different reasons and in a variety of ways. A bond developed between God and His children since He had carried them for so long. They trusted Him and knew He would not let them down. God carried them out of great love and compassion. Centuries have gone by, but the Lord still carries His children. This is a part of the joy of their journey. If I know the heart of my Father, he has great joy in His heart as He carries us.

## MY DREAM FOR MY SON

Many times people ask me what I want my son to do or be when he is grown. Most of them ask whether I have a desire for him to become a minister. "Brother Greg, I just imagine you cannot wait until you see Camden in the pulpit preaching someday, can you?" Others suggest, "Greg, have Boomer swinging a golf club at a young age. Why, Tiger Woods was hitting them when he was only a year old! You never know . . . he could be the next great golfer." Friends and family know how much I love Oklahoma Sooner athletics, so they mention about Camden starring at OU. "You probably have that boy passing the football every day, don't you? You just can't wait for him to go to OU and play football for the Sooners, can you?" Still others will say, "Lisa and you need to read to Camden all you can while he is young. You need to instill the desire for education in him early. He'll be able to make a lot of money some day, but it all begins when he is young."

What is my dream for my son? Actually my greatest desire for my son does not involve the University of Oklahoma and playing for the Sooners. When I served in Iowa Park, someone asked me, "Brother Greg, what would you do if Boomer went to the University of Texas and played quarterback for the Longhorns?" I replied, "I would be in the stands wearing burnt orange and cheering for him."

Nor does my greatest desire for him involve a great education and making a lot of money. Oh, sure, I want my son to have a good education and to live comfortably, but these are not my greatest desires. Nor do I dream that he will be golfing on the PGA tour someday. In fact my dream for Camden does not involve a calling into vocational ministry or preaching.

My greatest desire for my son is that, first and foremost, he has a relationship with God by trusting Jesus Christ as his personal Savior and Lord. I pray now for that special day when he will become a Christian. Early on we began teaching Him how special He is to God and that Jesus is God's Son. Two nights ago I asked Camden, "Who is Jesus?" To my delight he responded, "God's Son." My prayer is that one day the Holy Spirit will convict his little heart that he is a sinner. (His mother and I are well aware of this fact already!) My son's sin separates him from God. Yet God sent His Son, Jesus, to earth to become Camden's sin. Just for my boy, Jesus died an atoning death on the cross. I want my son to believe this and someday to trust Jesus Christ as his personal Savior.

The second part of my dream for my son is that he be all that God created him to become. I don't intend to sound trite with this statement. I sincerely mean it. God created Camden for a very special purpose. He is a miracle child. He was given to Lisa and me as a wonderful gift from God, but he was not given to us primarily. God placed him on this earth primarily because He has a tremendous plan for him. I don't know what that plan is, but when the time is right, God will reveal it to him. My great desire is that he follow God's plan for his life and that he fulfill each part of it perfectly. I can think of nothing better for my son. In the center of that plan will be where he finds the most joy and contentment this life will offer.

The ministers interviewed for this book expressed a similar longing for their children. I asked the group, "Which aspect of fatherhood brings you the most joy?" One-half of the entire group mentioned their children's faith in Christ or in seeing them fulfill God's plan for their lives. Interestingly the ministers whose children are now adults all mentioned their children's faith in Christ. One minister replied, "It is a great joy seeing your child embrace the same Christian values as an adult that you taught them as a child." I wish the same for my child. I want to free him to become whatever God has planned for his life.

A small church outside of Omaha, NE, was hosting an outdoor Bible conference. As he or she arrived, each person in the congregation was given a helium-filled balloon. The congregants were instructed to wait until the point in the service when their hearts were filled with joy and then at that moment release the balloon skyward. The act was to be a visible expression of their joy to the Lord. Throughout the inspirational service balloons were released at various points. Sadly, when the service concluded, more than one-third of the members of the congregation were still holding their balloons.[3]

So many of God's children go through life without joy, yet Jesus spoke often of how He desired His followers have it. My dream for Camden is to be all God created him to be and to live in the joy of his Heavenly Father. I want my boy to release his balloon often. My prayer is that my son not reach the end of life still clinging to his balloon.


## THAT MAGICAL MOMENT

One magical moment is indelibly etched in my mind. I pray it will be for the rest of my life. This one moment captures for me the 18 childless years, Camden's miraculous birth, and his first three years of life. As I conclude, allow me to recount this moment for you.

Earlier I mentioned a very special weekend for Camden and me when he was only 2. Lisa attended a women's retreat; Boomer and I were to be together for the weekend. I mentioned about the huge tears which ran down his cheeks when we kissed Mommy goodbye at the hotel and drove off. I recalled the wonderful events of the weekend. We played, sang, and spent every hour together. The weekend was very tiring but very rewarding and memorable.

We had been to McDonald's and had fun in the play area. In the restaurant we played hide-and-seek and other fun games. Both of us had a great time. Next we went to the park in Wylie, TX, to play soccer, basketball, and golf. We had been playing for several hours; we were both tired. "Boomer, it's time for us to go home and take a bath." He was tired, so he readily agreed.

I suggested we listen to a favorite CD and sing along as we drove home. His favorite CD contained children's songs to God. On our way home I placed this CD in the player and sang joyfully. The day was late; the sunset was the most beautiful I ever remember. Storm clouds had just missed us and moved on to the southwest. The sky was an awesome blend of purple and orange, with a setting sun barely peeking over the horizon. As we headed toward home, this beautiful sunset was just behind my son.

Just then, the song, "God Is So Good", began playing on the CD. He loves to sing along with the children's songs, so he began singing along. I looked at him in the rearview mirror and was simply stunned at what I saw. I saw this little angelic face with the most sincere expression singing, "God is so good, God is so good, God is so good, He's so good to me." In the background behind him was the most amazing sunset I think I have ever witnessed. Nature almost seemed to be in agreement with him; it seemed to serve as a backup singer testifying to the goodness of God.

I pulled over to the side of the road and simply stared into my rearview mirror at this amazing sight. Huge tears filled my eyes. One and then another fell. Soon tears were streaming down my face. A million thoughts raced through my mind at once: God's goodness to me . . . my salvation . . . giving me a loving wife and family . . . calling me into vocational service . . . giving me a great church in which to serve . . . and now the icing on the cake—a sweet little boy and the privilege of singing God's goodness with him. I am a blessed man. It was truly a magical moment. I joined in the song and began singing with him.

When the song concluded, I pulled back out onto the road to go home. I turned to my son and said, "Don't ever forget that, son. God is so good to you and me. He certainly is good to us!" He answered, "Yes."

And, once again, my eye saw Him.

# SCRIPTURE REFERENCES

(*Note: the references appear in the order they are mentioned in the chapter)

**Chapter 1**

John 8:32
Genesis 12:1-3
Genesis 18
Genesis 21
Job 1:1
Job 1:6
Job 1:12
Job 1:22
Job 38-41
Job 42:5
Isaiah 63:16
Ephesians 4:6
Isaiah 63:16
Ephesians 4:6
Isaiah 9:6
Jeremiah 3:19
2 Corinthians 6:18
Hebrews 1:5
Galatians 3:26
Galatians 4:7

**Chapter 2**

Genesis 12:2
Genesis 18
Genesis 21
Genesis 22:2-8
Genesis 11-12
Exodus 34:7
Deuteronomy 10:2
Deuteronomy 11:1
Deuteronomy 30:6
1 Kings 10:9
1 Chronicles 16:41
1 Chronicles 17:13
Matthew 5:44
Matthew 22:37
Luke 15
Romans 5:8
Romans 8:35-39
James 2:8
1 Peter 2:17
1 John 3:1
1 John 4:8
Psalm 139:13-15
John 10:28
John 3:16
Psalm 103:13-14

**Chapter 3**

Genesis 12
Genesis 37-50
Exodus 2
Joshua 24:15
Judges 6-8
Acts 13:22
Joel 2:11
Zechariah 6:15
Hebrews 5:8
Genesis 6:5-6
Exodus 32:1
Exodus 32:10
Matthew 17:16-17

**Chapter 4**

Ephesians 2:12
Ephesians 1:5
Romans 8:17
Galatians 4:7
Hebrews 1:2
1 Peter 3:7
Galatians 3:29
Ephesians 3:6
Ephesians 2:8-9
Luke 15
Deuteronomy 14:8
Job 1:8
Ephesians 6:4
Colossians 3:21
Exodus 32:10
Numbers 32:10
2 Kings 22:13
Numbers 14:18
Psalm 30:5
Psalm 86:15
Psalm 103:8
Matthew 7:8-11
James 1:17
2 Corinthians 9:15
Ephesians 2:8
Acts 2:38
Ephesians 4:8

Colossians 3:5
Romans 13:14
Colossians 2:11
Romans 8:8
2 Corinthians 5:17
John 8:32-34
Romans 5:12
Romans 5:20
Romans 6:11
Romans 6:14
Romans 6:22
Luke 19:10
Revelation 3:19
Deuteronomy 4:35-36
Psalm 94:12-13
Jeremiah 30:11
Jeremiah 46:28
Jeremiah 17:23
Jeremiah 32:33
Proverbs 1:7
Proverbs 3:11
Proverbs 10:17
Proverbs 23:23
Proverbs 19:18
Proverbs 29:17
Hebrews 12:5-11
James 1:17
1 John 4:10

## Chapter 10
Genesis 32
Genesis 28:15
Genesis 28:20-21
Genesis 31:49
Psalm 32:8
Psalm 66:7

Psalm 121:5-6
Isaiah 27:3
Jeremiah 24:6
Jeremiah 31:10
Philippians 1:20
Psalm 121:4
Ephesians 6:12
Isaiah 55:8-9
Psalm 125:2
Exodus 33:22
John 17:11
1 Peter 5:7
Psalm 57:1
Psalm 91:4
Psalm 25:4
Psalm 73:28
Psalm 145:18
Psalm 51:11
Jeremiah 23:23
Exodus 33:14
Deuteronomy 20:1
Isaiah 43:2
Genesis 22:1
Romans 8:28
2 Chronicles 25:8
Psalm 28:7
Psalm 40:17
Isaiah 41:10
Hebrews 13:6

## Chapter 11
Job 2:10
Job 38:2-3
Job 42:5
Hebrews 11:6

2 Corinthians
13:11-12
Genesis 3:8
Ezekiel 34:2
Revelation 1:15
Matthew 3:17
John 12:28-29
John 3:29
Acts 9:3-4

## Chapter 12
Psalm 127
Ephesians 6:4
Psalm 16:11
Nehemiah 8:10
Luke 10:21
John 15:11
John 16:24
John 17:13
Romans 14:7
Hebrews 12:2
1 Peter 1:8
Deuteronomy 30:9
Psalm 149:4
Isaiah 5:7
Isaiah 62:4
Isaiah 65:19
Jeremiah 31:20
Luke 1:14
Deuteronomy 1:31
Exodus 19:4
Deuteronomy
32:11
Isaiah 40:11
Isaiah 46:4

# SOURCES

### Chapter 1

1. Tom Bonfield. "$10,000 Babies." *The Cincinnati Enquirer*, April 17, 2005.
2. Alan H. DeCherney, Ed. "Fertility and Sterility." *A Journal of the American Society for Reproductive Medicine*, UCLA School of Medicine, Los Angeles, CA, 2006.
3. Raymond McHenry. *Quips, Quotes, and Other Notes*. Hendrickson Publishing, 1998. "Family."
4. McHenry. "Children."

### Chapter 2

1. Raymond McHenry. *Quips, Quotes, and Other Notes*. Hendrickson Publishing, 1998. "A Mother's Love."
2. Bonnie Keen. "Isaac." Sony/ATV Tunes. Cross Keys Publishing Co., 1998.
3. *Bible.org*. 2006. Sermon Illustrations: "Love of God." Source Unknown. *http://www.bible.org*

### Chapter 3

1. *Bits and Pieces*, May 28, 1992. p. 5-6
2. Dr. B.J. Miller. *Today in the Word*. November 1989, p. 11.

### Chapter 4

1. *Wikipedia*. August 3, 2006. "World War II." *http://www.wikipedia.com*
2. *Merriam-Webster Online Dictionary*. August 3, 2006. "ally." *http://www.merriam-webster.com*
3. *Wikipedia*. July 5, 2006. "John F. Kennedy." *http://www.wikipedia.com*

### Chapter 5

1. Hopeline. November 2, 1992. p. 4
2. Van Morrison. "Have I Told You Lately?" Avalon Records, 1989.
3. Clifton Fadiman. *The Little Brown Book of Anecdotes*. Random House Publishing, 1993.
4. *Houston Post*. July 18, 1994, p. A-9.

### Chapter 6

1. Howard Hendricks. *Teaching to Change Lives*. Multnomah Press, 2003. p. 66.
2. E.W. Bullinger. *Figures of Speech in the Bible*. Baker Book House, 1968. p. 881.
3. Lee Strobel. "God's Outrageous Claims." Seeds Tape Ministry. July 8, 1990.
4. Raymond McHenry. *McHenry's Quips, Quotes, and Other Notes*. Hendrickson Publishing, 1998. "Trust."
5. *Wikipedia*. July 14, 2006. "United States Declaration of Independence." *http://www.wikipedia.com*

**Chapter 7**

1. ESPN.Com. August 15, 2006. "The Most Memorable Moments of the Past 25 Years." Number 94. *http://www.espn.com*

2. *Wikipedia*. July 7, 2006. "Jeffrey Dahmer." *http://www.wikipedia.com*

3. Gordon Monson. "Weighing Compassion, Drive To Win." *Salt Lake Tribune*. August 9, 2006.

4. *Dads-daughters.com*. September 7, 2006. "Absentee Fathers: The Current State of Fatherhood." *http://www.dads-daughters.com*

5. Guy Greenfield. *The Wounded Parent*. Baker Book House, 1982.

**Chapter 8**

1. Larry Millett. Minnesota Historical Society. "David Kunst." July 17, 2002. *http://www.mnhs.org*

2. Babycenter. July 19, 2006. "Walking." *http://www.babycenter.com*

3. Alan Jackson. "Remember When." Arista Records, 2003.

4. Kenneth Barker, Gen. Ed. *The NIV Study Bible: New International Version*. "Assyria." Zondervan Publishing House, 1985.

5. Raymond McHenry. *McHenry's Quips, Quote,s and Other Notes*. Hendrickson Publishing, 1998. "Walking."

**Chapter 9**

1. *Bible.org* 2006. Sermon Illustrations: "Sin." *http://www.bible.org*

2. Charles Wesley. "Love Divine All Loves Excelling." 1747.

3. Raymond McHenry. *McHenry's Quips, Quotes, and Other Notes*. Hendrickson Publishing, 1998. "Sin Nature."

**Chapter 10**

1. Pony Express Home Station. 2006. "About The Pony Express." *www.xp-homestation.org*

2. Kidshealth: Nemours Foundation. July 20, 2006. "Sudden Infant Death Syndrome." Reviewed in September 2005 by Barbara P. Homeier, M.D. *www.kidshealth.org*

**Chapter 11**

1. *Wikipedia*. August 24, 2006. "Isidor Isaac Rabi." *www.wikipedia.com*

2. *Reader's Digest*. "Laughter Is The Best Medicine." November 1991.

3. *Tanbible.com*. 2006. *Hymn Stories*: "Trust and Obey." *www.tanbible.com*

4. *SBC.net*. 2006. *The Baptist Faith and Message*: The Scriptures." *www.sbc.net*

**Chapter 12**

1. Raymond McHenry. *McHenry's Quips, Quotes, and Other Notes*. Hendrickson Publishing, 1998. "Children."

2. Weekend Section. *USA Today*. July 15, 1994. p. 5.

3. *Bible.org*. 2006. Sermon Illustrations: "Joy." Bruce Larson. *www.bible.org*

# Family Album

At left, proud parents-to-be

Below left, Camden and I developed a bond quickly.

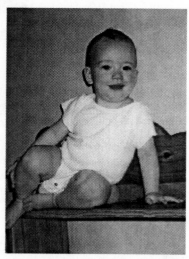

Above, sitting on his first pew

At right, in Iowa Park,
Camden enjoys his first snow.

Below, my father, Lee Roy, and
stepmother, Rose, hold their
infant grandson.

Above, wearing a tuxedo
in his first wedding to
attend

At left, a formal occasion
for both of us

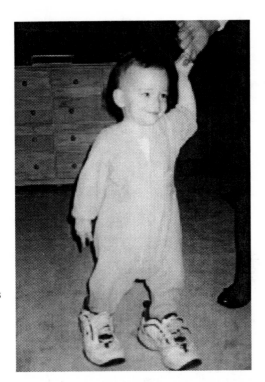

Walking in my shoes
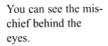

You can see the mis-
chief behind the
eyes.

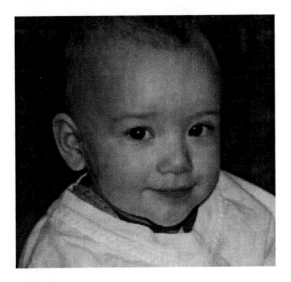

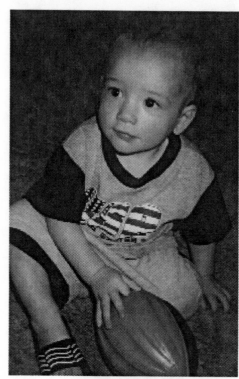

At left, Camden has always enjoyed sports.

Below, father and son

Above, Boomer enjoyed Christmas when he was a 2-year-old.

At left, he often says, "I want to wear a tie like Daddy."

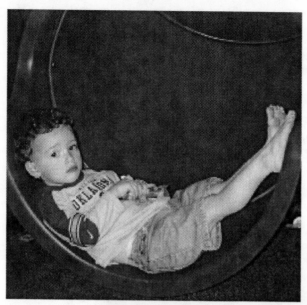

Above, relaxing in his
Sooner shirt as he plays on
the slide at McDonald's

At right, Christmas 2005

232

Camden and one
of his favorite cats

Eating the
forbidden fruit

At left, "Do we have to go to church?"

Below, Boomer enjoys dressing up.

234

Above, the Ammons family
Below, Camden has brought so much joy to our home.

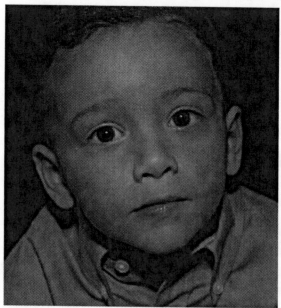

Above, Lisa, Camden,
and Greg Ammons in
the backyard
of their home


At left,
Camden "Boomer"
Ammons

# How to order more copies of
# *Now My Eye Sees You*

**by Greg Ammons**
**CALL: 1-800-747-0738**
**FAX: 1-888-252-3022**
**Email: orders@hannibalbooks.com**
**Write: Hannibal Books**
**P.O. Box 461592**
**Garland, Texas 75046**
**Visit:** *www.hannibalbooks.com*

Number of copies of *Now My Eye Sees You* _____

Multiply total number of copies: _____ by $12.95 =
Total cost of books: $_____

Add $3 for postage and handling for first book and add 50-cents for each additional book in the order.

Shipping total $_____
Texas residents add 8.25 % sales tax $_____

Total order $_____

number on check enclosed _____
credit card # _____ exp. date_____
(Visa, MasterCard, Discover, American Express accepted)

Name _____

Address _____

City State, Zip _____

Phone _____

Email _____

# Order directly from Hannibal Books

*Now My Eye Sees You* by Greg Ammons. A late-in-life, first-time father, though seminary-trained and a pastor for many years, gains unfathomable understanding about God when his son is born.

_____Copies at $12.95 =_____

*No Other Time Like This One* by Ed Jackson. Growing up in the 1940s in a small, West Texas town is capsuled in charming vignettes of high-school classmates whose lives reflect the era.

_____Copies at $9.95 = _____

*Way Back in the Country* by Kay Moore. Country recipes from six generations of an East Texas farm family encourage other families to preserve their own lore through cooking stories.

____Copies at $9.95 = _____

*When the Heart Soars Free* by Kay Moore. Christian fiction set in a ski lodge, where a storybook romance faces severe challenges that force main characters to learn about faith and forgiveness.

_____ Copies at $9.95 _____

*The Man in the Green Jeep*, by Viola Palmer. Global missions is personalized through this captivating glance into children's lives and culture in Central America.

_____Copies at $9.95 = _____

*Add $3.00 postage and handling for first book, 50 cents for each additional book.*

Shipping & Handling: _____

TX residents add 8.25% sales tax: _____

**Total Enclosed**
**(check or money order)** _____

Name _____

Address_____

City_____State_____Zip_____

Phone _____ Email _____

**See address and other contact information on page 237**

Printed in the United States
65507LVS00003B/127-600